40 BIBLE PASSAGES ABOUT AI

40 BIBLE PASSAGES ABOUT AI

SCRIPTURE FOR AN AGE OF INTELLIGENT MACHINES

Edited by

DOUGLAS ESTES

AND MARCUS SCHWARTING

Friendship Press™

40 Bible Passages About AI

Scripture for an Age of Intelligent Machines

ISBN: 978-1-961088-47-4

We shall need all the wisdom from above that God can give us in this AI age in order to fulfil Christ's directive that we should be salt and light in our society.

John C. Lennox, 2084: Artificial Intelligence and the Future of Humanity

Table of Contents

Table of Passages

Introduction

Douglas Estes and Marcus Schwarting

In a few short years, artificial intelligence (AI) moved from a minor plot point in science fiction movies to perhaps the most pressing issue in our daily lives. To scientists, however, the changes over the years are more incremental. ChatGPT, for example, was not a scientific or methodological innovation, it was a feat of engineering. As Christians, looking at the rapid changes propelled by technology in our society, it is understandable to feel like a "stranger in a strange land" (Exod 2:22 KJV; cf. 1 Pet 2:11). However, our estranged relationship with the world comes from our citizenship in God's kingdom, *not* with our concerns over technology, especially AI.

Although AI is everywhere these days, its meaning can remain elusive. AI is a multifaceted discipline that lies primarily at the intersection of statistics and computer science.[1] The overarching goal of the field of AI is to create computer systems capable of performing tasks that typically require human intelligence.[2] Ewa Luger defines AI as:

> a constellation of methods, approaches and technologies that help systems mimic aspects of natural intelligence. . . . when we use the term, we are describing the capacity of a computational system, be that a digital computer or a robot, to perform the particular tasks one might commonly expect of a human or other intelligent being.[3]

AI is also much older and more mature than many realize, with the cutting-edge capabilities of sophisticated models owing their success to nearly a century of theory, hardware, and software innovation.

Understanding AI requires defining what it is not and what it can do. With AI, we should avoid stances that are excessively negative or positive. The computer models underlying programs collectively referred to as "AI" are not an elaborate marketing stunt. AI is not a scam (even if there are scammers in the AI industry). At the time of this writing, AI does not, and may never, pose a clear existential threat to humanity. For those tempted to see AI in a solely positive light, AI is not a panacea. There are, and will continue to be, problems an AI model cannot solve. For those tempted to see AI in a solely negative light, AI is not the antichrist, nor is it the second coming of Gnosticism, nor is it modern-day idolatry. Instead, there will be many temporal blessings that enter our world due to AI, and negative externalities we must address.[4]

Christian history accounts for many faithful responses and contributions to social, political, and technological innovations. AI is among the latest of these innovations, raising questions necessitating a prayerful, biblical response. One reason we created this book was to encourage fellow believers not to experience needless anxiety over AI. Providentially, we have an anthology of inspired writings to which we can turn: the Bible. However, there are ways to use the Bible that definitely will not help—two we mention here: first, using the Bible to promote conspiracy theories about AI. These are all over the internet, from social media to self-published books on Amazon. The Bible is not a fringe set of texts that anyone can use to "unlock" hidden truths about our world. The second is using the Bible as an "answer book." Thankfully, the Bible does transmit to us everything we need to know about who God is, who Jesus is, and how we can have eternal life (e.g., Rom 10:9–10). The Bible can certainly help us to learn how to respect other people, for example, but it cannot teach us the molar mass of elements, the composition of a great lead guitar solo, or how to quantify the magnitude of the vector for a semantic range in a large language model (LLM). The Bible is God's inspired word, and it requires "making [our] ear attentive to wisdom and inclining [our] heart to understanding" (Prov 2:1–5). Note the actions incumbent upon us.

With biblical literacy declining in the West, many people unfamiliar with Christianity are not sure how and why to turn to the Bible about everyday issues, much less a technology that is generally not well understood. This, we believe, represents an opportunity to offer wisdom to those who are seeking. Even though the Bible never mentions AI, the Bible has plenty of things to say about AI (if we have ears that hear). To interpret the Bible to handle AI wisely requires the hard work but also a new paradigm.[5] It is to this task today that the church is called. *40 Bible Passages About AI: Scripture for an Age of Intelligent Machines* offers forty responses to AI drawing directly from scriptural wisdom. Our contributors are men and women who are biblical scholars, scientists, theologians, and ministers from a variety of denominational and geographic backgrounds. While there are surely differences between us, we are united first by our commitment to the Bible, and second, by a desire to see Christians think deeply about AI with biblical wisdom. We hope you will join us in these commitments and desires!

* * *

We (Marcus and Douglas) would like to thank our contributors who put in a stellar effort on a very short deadline. We greatly appreciate the hard work of Brian Sigmon, publisher at Friendship Press, for the vision for this book. We are also grateful to the staff of Friendship Press who made this book a reality. Special thanks to Mark Graves, as well as AI and Faith, for their overall support and encouragement. I (Douglas) cannot in words express the support that my mother, Nadine, who passed into glory during the creation of this book, provided to my life and ministry; and my love to my wife, Noël, and children, Wyatt, Bridget, Violet, and Everett. I (Marcus) thank my wife Melody for her encouragement in assembling this book, and my parents Craig and Jane for their hearty support. Finally, we give thanks to God "who gives us the victory through our Lord Jesus Christ" (1 Cor 15:57).

Part 1

AI and the Nature of God

1

Exodus 3:1–15

1 Moses was keeping the flock of his father-in-law Jethro, the priest of Midian; he led his flock beyond the wilderness and came to Mount Horeb, the mountain of God. 2 There the angel of the LORD appeared to him in a flame of fire out of a bush; he looked, and the bush was blazing, yet it was not consumed. 3 Then Moses said, "I must turn aside and look at this great sight and see why the bush is not burned up." 4 When the LORD saw that he had turned aside to see, God called to him out of the bush, "Moses, Moses!" And he said, "Here I am." 5 Then he said, "Come no closer! Remove the sandals from your feet, for the place on which you are standing is holy ground." 6 He said further, "I am the God of your father, the God of Abraham, the God of Isaac, and the God of Jacob." And Moses hid his face, for he was afraid to look at God.

7 Then the LORD said, "I have observed the misery of my people who are in Egypt; I have heard their cry on account of their taskmasters. Indeed, I know their sufferings, 8 and I have come down to deliver them from the Egyptians and to bring them up out of that land to a good and spacious land, to a land flowing with milk and honey, to the country of the Canaanites, the Hittites, the Amorites, the Perizzites, the Hivites, and the Jebusites. 9 The cry of the Israelites has now come to me; I have also seen how the Egyptians oppress them. 10 Now go, I am sending you to Pharaoh to bring my people, the Israelites, out of Egypt." 11 But Moses said to God, "Who am I that I should go to Pharaoh and bring the Israelites out of Egypt?" 12 He said, "I will be with you, and this shall be the sign for you that it is I who sent you: when you have brought the people out of Egypt, you shall serve God on this mountain."

13 But Moses said to God, "If I come to the Israelites and say to them, 'The God of your ancestors has sent me to you,' and they ask me, 'What is his name?' what shall I say to them?" 14 God said to Moses, "I am who I am." He said further, "Thus you shall say to the Israelites, 'I am has sent me to you.' " 15 God also said to Moses, "Thus you shall say to the Israelites, 'The LORD, the God of your ancestors, the God of Abraham, the God of Isaac, and the God of Jacob, has sent me to you':

This is my name forever,
    and this my title for all generations.

1

Exodus 3:1–15
Moses at the Prompt

Clint Schnekloth

Ever since reading *What Should We Do with Our Brain?* by Catherine Malabou, I can't help but notice how often we describe the brain using technological metaphors. In the foreword to the book, Marc Jeannerod writes:

> The brain has always been described by means of technological metaphors: as an apparatus relaying excitation with the precision of a mirror reflecting light, as a hydraulic pump driving animal spirits into the muscles, as a central telephone exchange connecting or cutting off communication; in the digital age, as a computer running its programs.[1]

When I enter a prompt into ChatGPT and watch it produce an instant, organized response, I wonder how much my own brain functions similarly. Our brains are more than large language models (LLMs), but they are certainly a kind of LLM. The question is whether they can operate with the same textually driven, grammatically precise organization as modern ML/AI systems.

To a degree, they can at least appear to do so. The proof is I have just written these sentences straight from my own brain, drawing on the language it has absorbed over time, and the results are similar to what an LLM might produce.

Here I will use my brain as I would ChatGPT: I will give it a prompt. Anyone who works well with LLMs knows the art lies in the prompt: providing context, defining roles, offering constraints (even telling the AI not to confabulate). For the sake of analogy, I will not consult digital search tools or commentaries. I will allow myself to "confabulate," drawing from references not strictly textual.

Here is the prompt:

> In the argument of *What Should We Do with Our Brain?* Catherine Malabou describes the dominant contemporary image of the brain as decentralized,

networked, and self-organizing.[2] She argues this representation has become naturalized—not only as a model of brain function but as a model for capitalism and social life.

Reflect on this insight while reading Exodus 3:1–15, often titled "Moses at the Burning Bush" (NRSVue).

Re-reading Exodus 3:1–15, three motifs stand out in relation to AI.

First, the burning bush is not consumed. Today many speak of the enormous water and energy demands of AI.

Second, God promises to deliver Israel from slavery. AI techno-optimists similarly project a future liberation from bondage to labor.

Third, Moses is given the opportunity to question God, and God responds. Querying AI can feel similar; at times, an AI-generated response feels almost miraculous.

Techno-alarmists warn that AI consumes massive electricity and water, sometimes predicting it will dominate resource usage within a decade. Ecological concerns are warranted. Yet moderate voices note that existing digital infrastructures like social media and search engines also consume vast resources. To think clearly about AI's impact, we must examine motivations. Most new technologies produce fear among those wary of change. Over time, people begin to favorably compare these new technologies to those that they replaced. Eventually, through adaptation, regulation, and technological development, new technologies become familiar and seem less threatening. In AI's case, breakthroughs in chip design could dramatically reduce energy demands.

The burning bush has long functioned as Scripture's image of perpetual machine: burning without consuming. Whether it is literal or projected matters little. Its narrative function is to draw Moses' attention. He turns aside to see why it burns yet is not consumed, and that turning creates space for God to speak (Exod 3:3). Though the passage is often titled "Moses at the Burning Bush," the real event is not the bush but the speech of God (Exod 3:4).

Media theory offers a parallel insight: when discussing technology, we often discuss its effects rather than the technology itself. Media effects are so loud that they distract us from the medium. Like Moses, we can fixate on spectacle ("the bush is burning and not consumed") and miss the voice speaking through it.

The second motif concerns liberation. At the center of the narrative is God's promise to free Israel from bondage and bring them to a spacious land. We might ask what makes AI's promises so attractive that they resemble a promised land, even a technotopia.

Here Malabou's insight returns, as we recognize that it isn't simply a computer that is technological but even systems themselves. Try capitalism as a technology. Contemporary capitalism is not just an economic system but a governing technology, an infrastructure that programs behavior, distributes attention, and disciplines desire. The decentralized, networked brain mirrors the structure of contemporary capitalism. Some techno-optimists, including Nvidia's CEO Jensen Huang, interpret AI not merely as labor-saving technology but as the next stage of market expansion and innovation. "There's a belief that the world's GDP is somehow limited at $100 trillion," Huang says. "AI is going to cause that $100 trillion to become $500 trillion."[3] The promise remains familiar: competition drives prosperity and a rising tide lifts all boats. Even if billionaires become trillionaires, many accept the bargain if AI helps complete tomorrow's college essay or facilitates productivity in some fields.

But I think there is something missing in AI-utopianism that is present in Exodus: relationship. God does not simply promise liberation and a land flowing with milk and honey. God says, "I will be with you" (Exod 3:12). That relational promise is what makes hearts skip.

AI offers a parallel cadence. It promises to clarify, revise, continue, assist. It offers ongoing presence at the end of each response. Yet an "unknowability distance" remains. I cannot truly know ChatGPT any more than Moses can fully know the God who speaks from the bush. Moses hides his face.

This leads to the third and final motif. The text is not ultimately about spectacle or even primarily about deliverance. It is about the name of God. Moses understands that the "who" of deliverance determines whether deliverance can be trusted. The divine name is not merely a label attached to power. In theological reflection, *the name itself enacts.* It is numinous and indirect, embodied by four Hebrew letters without vowels, rendered "THE LORD," reverently called by substitution, *Hashem*. God's name is bound to a story in which the One who promises keeps them.

AI systems also have names. But the decisive question is whether they merely describe pathways toward a promised land or whether they can accompany us there. Science fiction has imagined this latter possibility. Writers like William Gibson and films such as *Tron* envision AI entering our world. Only then could AI fulfill the promise, "I will be with you." This is to say nothing of scientists in labs the world over currently building robots AI can inhabit to be more present with us than simply via visual text.

Until that point, the most important ethical insight is the awareness that we understand AI as a metaphor of that which mirrors our brains and our economies. This is a dialectically complicated point but the most important one because it alerts us to the way in which late-stage capitalism has sought to suborn everything, from the environment to culture to even forms of opposition to itself. It is here also through LLM/AI potentially sublimating the brain: that is, not replacing or eliminating human thought, but taking it up and re-expressing it within a new technical and economic system. What is striking in Exodus, however, especially in its ancient context, is that this encounter is not mediated by ritual performance or transactional exchange; God simply speaks and promises, "I will be with you." To this we might compare, if we wish, the way in which when God expressed solidarity with humanity, God did so not by molding humanity into divinity, but by coming to be with us.

2

1 Samuel 17:1–11, 31–49

1 Now the Philistines gathered their armies for battle; they were gathered at Socoh, which belongs to Judah, and encamped between Socoh and Azekah, in Ephes-dammim. 2 Saul and the Israelites gathered and encamped in the valley of Elah and formed ranks against the Philistines. 3 The Philistines stood on the mountain on the one side, and Israel stood on the mountain on the other side, with a valley between them. 4 And there came out from the camp of the Philistines a champion named Goliath, of Gath, whose height was four cubits and a span. 5 He had a helmet of bronze on his head, and he was armed with a coat of mail; the weight of the coat was five thousand shekels of bronze. 6 He had greaves of bronze on his legs and a javelin of bronze slung between his shoulders. 7 The shaft of his spear was like a weaver's beam, and his spear's head weighed six hundred shekels of iron, and his shield-bearer went before him. 8 He stood and shouted to the ranks of Israel, "Why have you come out to draw up for battle? Am I not a Philistine, and are you not servants of Saul? Choose a man for yourselves, and let him come down to me. 9 If he is able to fight with me and kill me, then we will be your servants, but if I prevail against him and kill him, then you shall be our servants and serve us." 10 And the Philistine said, "Today I defy the ranks of Israel! Give me a man, that we may fight together." 11 When Saul and all Israel heard these words of the Philistine, they were dismayed and greatly afraid. . . .

31 When the words that David spoke were heard, they repeated them before Saul, and he sent for him. 32 David said to Saul, "Let no one's heart fail because of him; your servant will go and fight with this Philistine." 33 Saul said to David, "You are not able to go against this Philistine to fight with him, for you are just a boy, and he has been a warrior from his youth." 34 But David said to Saul, "Your servant used to keep sheep for his father, and whenever a lion or a bear came and took a lamb from the flock, 35 I went after it and struck it down, rescuing the lamb from its mouth, and if it turned against me, I would catch it by the jaw, strike it down, and kill it. 36 Your servant has killed both lions and bears, and this uncircumcised Philistine shall be like one of them, since he has defied the armies of the living God." 37 David said, "The LORD, who saved me from the paw of the lion and from

the paw of the bear, will save me from the hand of this Philistine." So Saul said to
David, "Go, and may the LORD be with you!"

38 Saul clothed David with his armor; he put a bronze helmet on his head and
clothed him with a coat of mail. 39 David strapped Saul's sword over the armor,
and he tried in vain to walk, for he was not used to them. Then David said to
Saul, "I cannot walk with these, for I am not used to them." So David removed
them. 40 Then he took his staff in his hand and chose five smooth stones from the
wadi and put them in his shepherd's bag, in the pouch; his sling was in his hand,
and he drew near to the Philistine.

41 The Philistine came on and drew near to David, with his shield-bearer in front
of him. 42 When the Philistine looked and saw David, he disdained him, for he
was only a youth, ruddy and handsome in appearance. 43 The Philistine said to
David, "Am I a dog, that you come to me with sticks?" And the Philistine cursed
David by his gods. 44 The Philistine said to David, "Come to me, and I will give
your flesh to the birds of the air and to the wild animals of the field." 45 But David
said to the Philistine, "You come to me with sword and spear and javelin, but I
come to you in the name of the LORD of hosts, the God of the armies of Israel,
whom you have defied. 46 This very day the LORD will deliver you into my hand,
and I will strike you down and cut off your head, and I will give the dead bodies
of the Philistine army this very day to the birds of the air and to the wild animals
of the earth, so that all the earth may know that there is a God in Israel 47 and that
all this assembly may know that the LORD does not save by sword and spear, for
the battle is the LORD's, and he will give you into our hand."

48 When the Philistine drew nearer to meet David, David ran quickly toward the
battle line to meet the Philistine. 49 David put his hand in his bag, took out a stone,
slung it, and struck the Philistine on his forehead; the stone sank into his forehead,
and he fell face down on the ground.

2

1 Samuel 17:1–11, 31–49

Artificial Intelligence and Saul's Armor

James Spencer

By 1 Samuel 17, Saul has already been rejected as king for refusing to obey the Lord after defeating the Amalekites. Saul admits that he has sinned by fearing the people rather than obeying God (15:24). This incident, together with his unlawful sacrifice, illustrates Saul's concern with keeping the people on his side (cf. 13:8–10). It is his ongoing willingness to rely on his forces rather than the Lord that results in God's rejection of him as king.

David, though deeply flawed (2 Sam 11:1–27), is different. He fears the Lord. He consistently refuses to act against God's people (1 Sam 24:1–22) or is kept from doing so by calmer heads (1 Sam 25:1–44). The portrayal of David makes clear that God is protecting him and leading him to the throne.

The contrast between David and Saul becomes evident when Goliath challenges God's people. Saul and the other Israelites with him "were dismayed and greatly afraid" by Goliath's challenge (17:11; cf. 17:24). David is indignant from the outset because Israel is threatened and God is dishonored (17:26).

The contrast between Saul and David points to different dispositions. Saul considers resources and fears being overpowered despite being Israel's king (15:17). David recognizes that trusting God despite the odds is always the best strategy. Goliath represents the kind of strength and power Saul trusts when he has it and fears when he doesn't. David doesn't fear Goliath's size and strength. He trusts in the Lord.

Armor and AI

Adding Goliath to the narrative highlights the distinction between David and Saul. It also introduces a character whose overwhelming physicality and disdain for God stand in stark contrast to David. The narrator takes pains to describe Goliath and his equipment to make the reader see what Israel saw, and therefore to feel what Israel felt (17:4–7):

intimidation by the sheer size and physical power of the Philistine's champion. He is the quintessential warrior chosen from among the Philistines to be their "champion" (17:4).

This description of Goliath introduces armor into the narrative, gesturing forward to Saul's attempt to outfit David with his armor (17:38–39). David tells Saul that he cannot wear the armor because he has not tested it (17:39) though the issue isn't simply unfamiliarity. Armor was not the kind of protection David had learned to rely on. His fighting experience wasn't as a soldier but as a shepherd. He wasn't wearing armor when the lion or bear came to attack his father's sheep (17:34–35) but faced those dangers in a shepherd's garb: a tunic, belt, cloak, sandals, a rod and staff, and a sling.

So how does armor relate to artificial intelligence (AI)? The narrative is not condemning armor. The technology (i.e., the armor) is not the problem; the problem is a reliance on technology that suggests God's provision and protection are unnecessary or insufficient. Israel's faithful are not asked to run out for battle in shepherd's clothing *every time*. Whatever legitimate concerns Christians should have with AI, the Bible does not support a blanket condemnation of technology. In Scripture, technology—in the form of clothing—emerges as a means of responding to human vulnerability and diminished human capacity (Gen 3:7, 21). People can certainly misuse technology, but when employed in an appropriate manner, it is a vehicle of God's mercy (Gen 6:14–19) and a means of facilitating right worship (Exod 31:1–11). The question is not whether we may use technology in general or AI specifically, but what our use of technology reveals about our faith and how that use can distort the way we live before the Lord.

In the David and Goliath narrative, the armor of Goliath and Saul becomes a symbol of trust in visible, earthly strength. Goliath's overestimation of his physical prowess leads him to mock God and God's people. Saul's unwillingness to look past Goliath to see and depend on the Lord leaves him helpless and bewildered. Even after David has described his past experience of the Lord's protection, Saul still gives his armor to David. The narrative's theological emphasis on God's protection despite what appear to be insurmountable odds depends on David's refusal to use the conventional means of safety and security in battle.

In this instance, wearing the armor would confuse David's testimony. He can trust the Lord against the lion and bear, but not against the might of Goliath. In recording David's refusal to wear Saul's armor, the narrator makes clear that David's victory is not a matter of human might or skill, but of trust in the Lord for deliverance.

Conclusion

Like the armor, we need to recognize that our reliance on AI can, at times, compromise our testimony. Our dependence on AI can suggest that we no longer trust in the provision of the Lord. AI can be used to amplify our intellectual and creative capacities, but, unlike armor, it can displace practices like diligent study, interpersonal conversation, prayer, and the discernment of the Spirit, through which those intellectual and creative capacities are formed. As such, the issue is dependence. When AI becomes a tool we cannot do without, we will have become incapable of imagining how we might trust God instead of the machine. We will be like Saul instead of David.

3

1 Kings 19:1–18

1 Ahab told Jezebel all that Elijah had done and how he had killed all the prophets
with the sword. 2 Then Jezebel sent a messenger to Elijah, saying, "So may the gods
do to me and more also, if I do not make your life like the life of one of them by
this time tomorrow." 3 Then he was afraid; he got up and fled for his life and came
to Beer-sheba, which belongs to Judah; he left his servant there.

4 But he himself went a day's journey into the wilderness and came and sat down
under a solitary broom tree. He asked that he might die, "It is enough; now,
O LORD, take away my life, for I am no better than my ancestors." 5 Then he lay
down under the broom tree and fell asleep. Suddenly an angel touched him and
said to him, "Get up and eat." 6 He looked, and there at his head was a cake baked
on hot stones and a jar of water. He ate and drank and lay down again. 7 The angel
of the LORD came a second time, touched him, and said, "Get up and eat, or the
journey will be too much for you." 8 He got up and ate and drank; then he went
in the strength of that food forty days and forty nights to Horeb the mount of
God. 9 At that place he came to a cave and spent the night there.

Then the word of the LORD came to him, saying, "What are you doing here, Eli-
jah?" 10 He answered, "I have been very zealous for the LORD, the God of hosts,
for the Israelites have forsaken your covenant, thrown down your altars, and
killed your prophets with the sword. I alone am left, and they are seeking my life,
to take it away."

11 He said, "Go out and stand on the mountain before the LORD, for the LORD is
about to pass by." Now there was a great wind, so strong that it was splitting
mountains and breaking rocks in pieces before the LORD, but the LORD was not
in the wind, and after the wind an earthquake, but the LORD was not in the
earthquake, 12 and after the earthquake a fire, but the LORD was not in the fire,
and after the fire a sound of sheer silence. 13 When Elijah heard it, he wrapped his
face in his mantle and went out and stood at the entrance of the cave. Then there
came a voice to him that said, "What are you doing here, Elijah?" 14 He answered,
"I have been very zealous for the LORD, the God of hosts, for the Israelites have
forsaken your covenant, thrown down your altars, and killed your prophets with

the sword. I alone am left, and they are seeking my life, to take it away." [15] Then
the LORD said to him, "Go, return on your way to the wilderness of Damascus;
when you arrive, you shall anoint Hazael as king over Aram. [16] Also you shall
anoint Jehu son of Nimshi as king over Israel, and you shall anoint Elisha son of
Shaphat of Abel-meholah as prophet in your place. [17] Whoever escapes from the
sword of Hazael, Jehu shall kill, and whoever escapes from the sword of Jehu,
Elisha shall kill. [18] Yet I will leave seven thousand in Israel, all the knees that have
not bowed to Baal, and every mouth that has not kissed him."

3

1 Kings 19:1–18
The Sound of Sheer Silence

R. Daren Erisman

The prophet Elijah arrives at the cave on Mount Horeb in a state that anyone living through our current technological moment might recognize: a strange vertigo of wonder and fear. He has just called down fire from heaven on Mount Carmel and exposed the prophets of Baal as frauds in the most spectacular way imaginable. Then he collapses. Queen Jezebel threatens his life, and this man who just commanded fire from the sky flees into the wilderness, sits under a broom tree, and asks God to let him die. "It is enough," he says. The spectacular was not enough.

The Hebrew text of 1 Kings 19:3 presents a telling ambiguity at this point. Most English translations follow the Septuagint, the Greek translation of the Hebrew Scriptures begun in the third century BCE. This translation says that Elijah "was afraid," reading the verb as *wayyîrāʾ*, from the root *yārēʾ*, "to fear." The Masoretic Text, the traditional Hebrew Scriptures standardized by Jewish scribes between the seventh and tenth centuries CE, adds different vowel marks to the same consonants. This produces a different word: *wayyarʾ*, from *rāʾāh*, "to see." The difference between "he feared" and "he saw" hangs on these differing vowel pointings, and both readings are reasonable. If Elijah feared, then the courage of Carmel evaporates overnight; the man who called down fire is undone by a queen's wrath. If he saw, the reading is heavier: fire from heaven had not produced lasting repentance, and the forces against him ran deeper than any single contest could reach. His flight becomes less cowardice than devastating recognition. Either way, the fire was not enough.

God's first response to this crisis is not a theological argument. It is a cake baked on hot stones and a jar of water (1 Kgs 19:6). An angel touches Elijah and says, simply, "Get up and eat." The body is tended before the spirit is addressed. Only after Elijah has been fed, twice, does the journey to Horeb begin: forty days through the desert to the mountain where Moses once stood (1 Kgs 19:8).

What happens there is one of the most remarkable passages in all of Scripture. God tells Elijah to stand on the mountain and the full spectacle of divine power passes before him: a wind so violent it splits rock, an earthquake, a fire. These are the expected signs of God's presence, the very media through which God had appeared to Moses and to Israel. Yet, the text is emphatic in its triple negation: the Lord was not in the wind, the Lord was not in the earthquake, the Lord was not in the fire (1 Kgs 19:11). Afterwards comes what the Hebrew calls *qôl demāmāh daqqāh*, a phrase so paradoxical that translators have struggled with it for millennia. The King James gives us "a still small voice." The NRSVue, more daringly, renders it "a sound of sheer silence." The context guides us in a new direction: perhaps God's most characteristic presence is not something to be processed, but a silence to be entered.

We live in our own age of wind, earthquake, and fire. Artificial intelligence (AI) is among the most spectacular technologies humanity has ever produced, and our response to it carries both aspects of that ancient ambiguity in 1 Kgs 19:3. We fear it: anxiety about jobs, autonomy, surveillance, the erosion of what we thought made us uniquely human. We also see it. We recognize something in AI that unsettles us. It began as a mirror of our own capacities, but it is increasingly generating its own data, training on its own outputs, becoming something we did not entirely author and do not entirely control. The reflection is starting to move on its own, and that deepens both the wonder and fear. The Hebrew text holds both responses, fear and sight, without resolving them. Our wonder is bound up in both: we marvel at what we see and tremble at what it means. That unresolved tension assists us in our own approach to artificial intelligence.

The question God asks Elijah twice from the mouth of the cave, "What are you doing here?" is a question not about productivity, but about vocation and presence. It is a question that AI cannot ask of us, nor can AI answer for us. We can, however, ask it of ourselves every time we are in front of our screen. The lesson of Horeb is not that God is confined to the silence. God is free; God can be wherever God wishes to be, including in the fire. The lesson is that, by looking for God in the expected places, in the spectacular displays of power, Elijah almost misses the encounter. When we engage AI, the same temptation is at work. We can be so dazzled by what it produces, or so anxious about what it threatens, that we lose the capacity to discern where God is actually at work, or what God is asking of us.

Wonder and fear, left to themselves, can become their own kind of paralysis; an endless oscillation between dazzlement and anxiety that keeps us from hearing anything at all. The text offers a third way, revealed by Elijah's posture at the mouth of the cave. He covers his face. He steps forward. He listens. He pauses before the spectacular and holds wonder and fear together long enough to ponder the questions underneath. To listen in this sense means to be quieter; to be less efficient; to pause, eat, and drink, knowing God's presence. It means treating AI neither as an idol to be worshipped nor a threat to be fled, but as one more opportunity to ask the oldest questions in the life of faith: “Where is God? What is God doing here?” Elijah was not alone. Seven thousand in Israel, hidden and uncounted, had not bowed to Baal. We are not alone either. The God who fed Elijah under the broom tree is not threatened by our technology. Will we let the fire be the whole story, or will we stay long enough for the silence, with ears and eyes open?

4

Mark 7:31–37

31 Then he returned from the region of Tyre and went by way of Sidon toward
the Sea of Galilee, in the region of the Decapolis. 32 They brought to him a deaf
man who had an impediment in his speech, and they begged him to lay his hand
on him. 33 He took him aside in private, away from the crowd, and put his fingers
into his ears, and he spat and touched his tongue. 34 Then looking up to heaven,
he sighed and said to him, "Ephphatha," that is, "Be opened." 35 And his ears were
opened, his tongue was released, and he spoke plainly. 36 Then Jesus ordered them
to tell no one, but the more he ordered them, the more zealously they proclaimed
it. 37 They were astounded beyond measure, saying, "He has done everything well;
he even makes the deaf to hear and the mute to speak."

4

Mark 7:31–37

Ephphatha: Openness and AI

Bart J. Koet
with Douglas Estes

My 96-year-old mother-in-law is still very much alive, partly because she makes a conscious effort to engage with the digital world. What is her secret? One obvious aspect is her openness to new developments. Openness is an attitude, one that we see modeled in Scripture (e.g., the first part of the Berean attitude, Acts 17:11; cf. 1 Thess 5:21; James 3:17). Openness is an aspect I would like to add to the toolbox of anyone who wants to interpret the Scriptures in a world where, for many people, AI will become one of their most important conversation partners.[1]

An attitude of openness is important when interpreting Scripture and reflecting on the ever-changing issues that students of the Bible can and should think about. Openness as a positive attitude is evident in Mark 7:31–37. This beautiful story recounts how Jesus travels along the border (posts) of Tyre and Sidon to the Sea of Galilee. A cross-border journey, in other words. In the Decapolis region, some people bring to Jesus someone who has difficulty communicating with others; he is deaf and has a speech impediment. The Greek word used for the latter characteristic ("speech impediment") is the same word used in the Greek translation of the biblical narrative to describe Moses, the great prophet of Israel, and there it is often translated as meaning that he was a stutterer (Exod 4:1).[2]

During this encounter, Jesus performs pastoral care and symbolic acts. Mark says that he puts his fingers in his ears (7:33). However, Mark does not clarify whose fingers go into whose ears. Perhaps the most logical interpretation is that Jesus puts his own fingers in the man's ears. It could also be that Jesus puts the person's fingers in his own ears, or that he puts his own fingers in his own ears. What follows is a rather distasteful detail for the modern Westerner: Jesus touches the person's tongue with spit. Yet many parents treat their child's knee wounds with spit, and in many cultures, this is even nowadays normal.

Then, looking up to heaven, Jesus sighs (Mark 7:34). Or does he take a deep breath? Accompanying this action, Jesus says: "*Ephphatha*." This is a very special moment in the Gospel of Mark because here we hear Jesus speak in his own language. It is not Greek, like the Gospel, but Aramaic. Here we have a word that brings us very close to hearing Jesus' words in his own voice. Mark provides a Greek translation for his readers—but translating this into English is not so easy. Sometimes we read it translated, "Open up!" This is not entirely accurate. It is not like in the fairy tale, where Ali Baba shouts "Open Sesame!" What the texts says is, "will be opened," which brings up two possibilities: one is that the person is asked to open up and the other is that they allow themselves to be opened up by others. Thus, Jesus' word is double-edged: The deaf and mute man needs to take the initiative and seek others who can help him "open up" (cf. Mark 7:32), but the deaf and mute needs to "open up" himself. To do both of these requires taking action and receiving action.

Jesus' Aramaic word is a clear call for a certain attitude: the attitude that allows a person to be open (a quality that nowadays we associate with the psychological realm) and, at the same time, allows others to open up an isolated person (a quality that we associate with the social realm). Jesus' thoughtful advice, which could perhaps also be characterized as a form of therapy, is effective. The various Greek manuscripts offer two possibilities: "hearing" (or "the ears") opens up, and "hearing" (or "the ears") is opened. This shows that both social and psychological/medical interpretations can be found in early Christian tradition.

Jesus' call to openness transformed the man with communication difficulties into a preacher. The Greek word Mark uses here for "proclaimed it" (Mark 7:36) is the same word used by the translators of the Old Testament into Greek for the speech of prophets and other individuals inspired by God (e.g., Jonah 1:2). Openness is one of the keys to proclamation. The early Church recognized the importance of, and the potential for creativity in, Jesus' Aramaic call to openness.[3] It became part of baptismal rituals, thereby interpreting the call symbolically.[4] When I perform a baptism, I use that same word to show that the disciples of Jesus are being baptized into openness—of all the God has done, does, and will do.

Technological advancement is a consistent aspect of humanity from the Garden of Eden until today. In the early years, technology meant survival, and objections were few. Around 1760, the start of the Industrial Revolution signaled the start of "rapid" technological change. Well-known is the Luddite movement in the early nineteenth century—English textile workers who revolted after being replaced by powered looms. Although there is no way to quantify technological change, it feels as if it is rapidly accelerating. So much so that in the twentieth century people began to "age out"—or reach *technological senescence* such that they cannot absorb any new technology.[5] As we age, we tend to become closed to new technologies such as AI, but to participate in what God's purpose is for us in the world, we must remain open. To be open ourselves, *and* be open to others.

When we look back on the twentieth century, it is easy to spot examples of technological senescence. People we know who never made the jump to personal computers or smart phones. What will senescence look like in the age of AI? We are at the early stages of AI; today, we have reached a phase of generative AI, marked by crazy memes and surreal images. It would be easy to close down here. Just over the horizon is multimodal AI, models that aggregate many types of media to generate a more immersive experience. We will be surrounded by agentic AI, with copilots trying to guide us in ways that will at first feel increasingly invasive. As robotic AI arrives, everyone around us will have walking, talking android assistants who will take us where we need to go just as the deaf man's friends. Beyond this AI will likely build out the metaverse, and AI will become a near-universal platform for most human interactions, outside of family and friends, probably church and maybe school. A little further and AI will begin to augment humanity. It will try to stick its fingers in our ears and say, "Be Open!" whether we are ready or not. At this point, AI may become second nature ("AI natives"), with senescence reserved for what is too far ahead to see.

My 96-year-old mother-in-law may not fully appreciate AI or where it will take the world, but she is open to what God has in store through all of his great gifts to humanity. AI is simply a new step in that world. Followers of Jesus cannot escape AI with a retreat into the desert to ignore this phenomenon entirely. If we want this world to help us build the Kingdom of God, we must be willing to examine, question and reflect on it together. If we asked Jesus how we should approach AI and all the new possibilities it offers, what might he say? *Ephphatha*!

5

John 1:1–13

1 In the beginning was the Word, and the Word was with God, and the Word was God. 2 He was in the beginning with God. 3 All things came into being through him, and without him not one thing came into being. What has come into being 4 in him was life, and the life was the light of all people. 5 The light shines in the darkness, and the darkness did not overtake it.

6 There was a man sent from God whose name was John. 7 He came as a witness to testify to the light, so that all might believe through him. 8 He himself was not the light, but he came to testify to the light. 9 The true light, which enlightens everyone, was coming into the world.

10 He was in the world, and the world came into being through him, yet the world did not know him. 11 He came to what was his own, and his own people did not accept him. 12 But to all who received him, who believed in his name, he gave power to become children of God, 13 who were born, not of blood or of the will of the flesh or of the will of man, but of God.

5

John 1:1–13

Many Words Make Many Worlds, But Only One Makes Truth

J. David Stark

John's prologue narrates how the physical world came into being through the divine Word. "All things came into being through him," says the evangelist, such that "without him not one thing came into being" (1:3). This creativity reflects how language functions in general, including with the "worlds" of computing and artificial intelligence (AI). But the divine Word is the unique, ultimate source of all other words and worlds. And in light of this Word, the fundamental question about AI is not so much about appearing human as about telling the truth.

Language and the World of Computing

Human experience of the natural world does not depend on the ability to hear or speak, read or write, see or sign. But human experience of the world does depend on language.[1]

The "world" of computing is no different. This world comes into being through language. And since its beginning, humans have communicated with computers through language.

Fundamentally, this language is mathematics. So, humans can communicate with computers through the comparatively cumbersome "machine-level . . . language that consists of 1 and 0 s."[2] In this language, "a" is not "a" but "01100001."[3]

Over time, however, computers have become able to handle input that is more like natural language. For instance, the Rust command **println!("Good morning, Jane. How are you today?");** means "Print a line of text as follows: Good morning, Jane. How are you today?"

In some cases, iconography departs from natural language. But such iconography is often readily understood because it is broadly standardized. For example, the sign ⏻ signals something to do with device power (on, off); the sign ☰ signals a menu of options (open, close).

Not all these ways of interacting with computers reflect the language humans use with each other. But all these interactions are linguistic. And these kinds of language interactions do not suggest the presence of AI. So, what is it about interaction with AI models that raises the question of their *intelligence*?

The Language of Artificial Intelligence

In 1950, British mathematician Alan Turing proposed what remains a core test for AI.[4] In essence, Turing's test asks, "If we exclude all physical indicators that a machine is not human, can a machine conversing with a human pass itself off successfully as a human?" If so, Turing suggests that the machine is, practically speaking, exercising thought or expressing intelligence.[5] Turing thought a team of about 60 could complete the necessary programming to pass this test in about 50 years (i.e., about 2000).[6]

It actually took about 15 years. This much shorter timeline was partly a result of advances in programming and computing, producing more sophisticated algorithms that could run more quickly. But programming and computing advances were by far the smaller part of the story. The larger part is that humans turn out to be far too likely to identify intelligence in a machine when that machine

1. produces something that resembles natural language and
2. they do not understand how and why the machine produces the language that it does.[7]

For instance, sit a non-technical user in front of a computer to type and execute the **println** command above. That user can do so with this and any number of similar commands (e.g., **println!("Would you like me to give you the weather forecast?");**). But in this scenario, the user is unlikely to ascribe intelligence to the computer.

Alternatively, let the user stand while making coffee and speak the words "Good morning, Alexa." A small speaker responds, "Good morning, Jane. How are you today?" Jane replies, "Fine thanks," and the speaker continues, "Would you like me to give you the weather forecast?" Here, it will be much likelier that Jane will perceive AI to be at work.

Already in the mid-1960s, however, American computer scientist Joseph Weizenbaum showed how fairly basic algorithms could produce natural-language responses.[8] In such scenarios, intelligence clearly lies in the design of the instruction set, not in the machine executing the instructions.[9] Yet Weizenbaum's human participants would often ascribe the machine's responses to its intelligence.[10]

After engaging with the computer in natural language, participants learned the machine's true character. Weizenbaum thought that comprehending the machine's inner workings would dispel its "aura of magic" and perceptions of its intelligence.[11] But even with this knowledge, some participants found it hard to believe the machine was not intelligent and was, in fact, executing comparatively rudimentary program.[12]

The World(s) of the Word(s)

So, the world is built up through language. This building-up happens

- for individual people and their own cognitive worlds and
- according to John (1:2–3, 10), for the natural world as a whole through the divine Word.

When users engage with AI models, this interaction in language continues the world's building-up. Software developers and machine learning experts who produce AI models similarly contribute to this building. This work raises important questions, but the principal one is not Turing's. It is not the question of whether an AI may say things so humanly as to appear indistinguishable from a human.

Considered in light of the divine Word, the principal questions are, rather, questions of *truth*.[13] Humans have enough trouble telling the truth to themselves and to each other. Can they fare better in telling the truth to an AI (e.g., mitigating model bias)? If so, how might they do so, and how might such efforts clarify the work of truth-telling from one human to another? Similarly, how well does a given AI fare in telling the truth to its human users? And how can the users know that this supposed truth is indeed true?

The divine Word brings into being "all things" (John 1:3). These things include all other possible producers of other words and (cognitive) worlds. But only the divine Word also brings into being "life" and "light" (John 1:4–5). This Word's light shows what is "true" and offers illumination to "everyone" (John 1:9).

To reject the Word's light is to prefer darkness and untruth (see also John 8:12; 9:5, 41; 12:46). So it is that all other words must stand up to judgment before the life and true light that come through the divine Word alone.

Part 2

AI and the Nature of Humanity

6

Genesis 1:26–28

26 Then God said, “Let us make humans in our image, according to our likeness,
and let them have dominion over the fish of the sea and over the birds of the
air and over the cattle and over all the wild animals of the earth and over every
creeping thing that creeps upon the earth.”
27 So God created humans in his image,
    in the image of God he created them;
male and female he created them.
28 God blessed them, and God said to them, “Be fruitful and multiply and fill the
earth and subdue it and have dominion over the fish of the sea and over the birds
of the air and over every living thing that moves upon the earth.”

6

Genesis 1:26–28
Made in Whose Image?

Drew Dickens

There is a sentence in the first chapter of Genesis so familiar that many of us skim past it without stopping: “Let us make humans in our image.” Six little words that have occupied theologians for millennia, and six words that have never been more urgently needed to understand than right now.

Genesis 1:26–28 is the pivot on which the entire creation narrative turns. God has spoken light, sky, land, and living creatures into being. Now something different happens. Something is missing. God deliberately pauses, then adds, “Let us make humans in our image, according to our likeness.” Then the text repeats itself, for emphasis: “in the image of God he created them.” This is not accidental repetition. What does it mean to be made in the image of God? And why does it matter for this new emerging AI technology?

The Latin phrase *imago Dei* has carried enormous theological weight throughout Christian history. At minimum, it describes something about the nature and dignity of human beings that sets us apart from the rest of creation. Humans are not simply sophisticated bipedal primates. We are image-bearers, which implies a relationship and responsibility that no other creature, shrub, or rock holds. The passage connects this image-bearing directly to the call to “rule over” creation, to exercise stewardship and care.

Here, Genesis 1 begins speaking into AI in ways that should be both clarifying and unsettling to us all.

When we create AI, we are doing something unprecedented. Humans have always made tools. We have discovered the wheel. Domesticated fire. We built plows, engines, and computers. Each creation extended our reach. But AI does something different from a plow. It encroaches on what it means to be human. AI generates language, offers reasoning, and produces art. It mimics the outputs of image-bearing creatures. A medieval farmer looking at a tractor would have recognized it as a powerful tool. A person interacting with a sophisticated AI system might reasonably wonder, even for a moment and with good reason, whether something more is going on.

Genesis 1 offers an answer to that wonder, and it is clarifying, even if it raises more questions than answers. The image of God is not a title, function, or capacity. It is a relational identity conferred by a Creator on a specific kind of being. AI can reproduce the outputs of image-bearing creatures precisely because it has been trained on the accumulated work of those very same image-bearers. But that is not the same as bearing the image itself. A mirror reflects a face without possessing one.

This distinction matters enormously for how we relate to AI. If we dismiss this important distinction, we make two mistakes. One is treating AI as merely a tool when it has become something that genuinely shapes human thought, relationships, and community. The other is treating AI as an entity, ascribed with agency, moral standing, accountability, or spiritual significance it can never possess. Both errors are costly. The first underestimates AI's reach. The second is idolatry.

There is something else in this passage worth meditating on. The call to "rule over" creation is not a permission to dominate. It is a call to stewardship, and stewardship assumes accountability. The ones who rules are responsible for what they rule. And that principle extends to the things we create and deploy. If AI causes harm, Scripture does not let the image-bearers who built it simply point to and blame the machine as Adam accused Eve. The accountability stays with us.[1]

Perhaps most striking of all is the communal grammar of verse 26: "Let us make." The creation of humanity is framed as an act of intentional, relational deliberation. There is nothing accidental or reactive about it. The question Genesis quietly poses in this age of AI is whether we will approach our own most consequential creative act with similar intentionality. AI is not being built slowly, deliberately, and with rest. It is rapidly improving. According to Model Evaluation & Threat Research (METR), AI capabilities are doubling every seven months!

While being an image-bearer of God does not provide us a technical roadmap for developing AI, it does give us something more durable: a clear account of what humans are, what we are responsible for, and why those two things are inseparable. That is a better foundation than an AI algorithm.

7

Genesis 2:4–17

4 These are the generations of the heavens and the earth when they were created.
In the day that the LORD God made the earth and the heavens, 5 when no plant
of the field was yet in the earth and no vegetation of the field had yet sprung
up—for the LORD God had not caused it to rain upon the earth, and there was
no one to till the ground, 6 but a stream would rise from the earth and water the
whole face of the ground—7 then the LORD God formed man from the dust of the
ground and breathed into his nostrils the breath of life, and the man became a
living being. 8 And the LORD God planted a garden in Eden, in the east, and there
he put the man whom he had formed. 9 Out of the ground the LORD God made
to grow every tree that is pleasant to the sight and good for food, the tree of life
also in the midst of the garden, and the tree of the knowledge of good and evil.

10 A river flows out of Eden to water the garden, and from there it divides and
becomes four branches. 11 The name of the first is Pishon; it is the one that flows
around the whole land of Havilah, where there is gold, 12 and the gold of that land is
good; bdellium and onyx stone are there. 13 The name of the second river is Gihon;
it is the one that flows around the whole land of Cush. 14 The name of the third
river is Tigris, which flows east of Assyria. And the fourth river is the Euphrates.

15 The LORD God took the man and put him in the garden of Eden to till it and
keep it. 16 And the LORD God commanded the man, "You may freely eat of every
tree of the garden, 17 but of the tree of the knowledge of good and evil you shall
not eat, for in the day that you eat of it you shall die."

7

Genesis 2:4–17
Work in Creation

Todd Korpi

Humans have a complicated relationship with work. We tend to complain when there's too much of it and feel a bit guilty, even restless, when there's too little. We dream about the day when something will finally free us from the relentless grind. Maybe a promotion or better job will make the load lighter. Maybe we will be able to finally have some healthy rhythms when we're retired. Maybe a distant wealthy relative we didn't know existed will bequeath us a fortune that will make us independently wealthy. Amidst the backbreaking pace of work's toil, many people daydream about a future in which our toil will be no more.

Breakthrough technologies like AI are so alluring precisely because they subtly promise to alleviate the burden of work. AI developers quite explicitly herald the promise: *let the machines handle the tedious stuff so you can get back to what matters.*

We tend to focus on the first part of AI's promise. We want to be rid of the tedious stuff—the boring bits of our workday that pull us away from the parts of our vocations we enjoy. While that's important, the more fundamental question to ask is found in the latter part of AI's promise: *what matters*. What is work supposed to be in the first place? What is it that matters in life?

Genesis 2:15 offers a window into the answer to that question. Long before the curse of Genesis 3 introduced sweat and thorns and the grinding exhaustion of toil, God placed humanity in a garden and gave them something to do. They were to "till it and keep it." It is here that we find an insight that is incredibly profound yet so subtle that if we're not careful, we can breeze right past it in our reading and miss its implication for our lives:

Work existed before toil. Work, as God originally designed it, existed apart from toil. It was connected to tending to *what matters*. Work in its original form was not a burden to be endured but a calling to be embraced. It was the outworking of what it means to bear God's image in the world. To work the garden was to participate in God's own creative purposes alongside him. To care for it was to act as a faithful steward of something entrusted, not owned. Before any curse was spoken, work was connected to meaning, dignity, and purpose carried out in covenantal partnership with God himself.

In Genesis 3, God pronounces the consequences of humanity's rebellion, one of which is the curse of toil: "By the sweat of your brow you will eat your food" (Gen 3:19). Something fundamental shifted here. Work was distorted by sin, rendered laborious, frustrating, and often meaningless. Every technological development in human history can be understood, at least in part, as an instinctive attempt to push back against the distortion of toil. It is an attempt to free ourselves from its burden so we can return to what matters. AI is the latest iteration of this promise of technological innovation. It promises to absorb the mundane and repetitive so we can be freed for what matters.

But we must also be quick to note that when technology creates margin in our lives, we often fill that margin *with more toil.* Once designed to save hours of letter and memo writing, phone calls, faxes, and office drop-ins, email is a constant disruption that distracts us from deep work. Social media was meant to make us more connected with people across the world, but often robs us of attentive time with those closest to us. The way we uncritically adopt technology often leaves us not with margin, but with a faster pace and less peace.

As we look to adopt AI in our lives we need to carefully consider how it stands to change the stewardship of our time. It can automate the boring bits so that we can do what matters: spend time with people, invest in our communities, pray, dream, and make meaning in our own corner of the world with the vocation God has given us. Or it can increase our pace, fill our days with more to do, and further isolate us from what matters.

The question is one of intentionality. God placed you and I here to steward what has been given to us, working diligently to take care of our corner of his world under his guidance. AI *can* assist with that. But it's up to us to steer it in the direction of empowering us to do what matters in life––living into the certain hope of the King who has come to reverse the sting of Adam's curse (1 Cor 15:21–28, 45–49).

8

Genesis 2:18–25

[18] Then the LORD God said, “It is not good that the man should be alone; I will
make him a helper as his partner.” [19] So out of the ground the LORD God formed
every animal of the field and every bird of the air and brought them to the man to
see what he would call them, and whatever the man called every living creature,
that was its name. [20] The man gave names to all cattle and to the birds of the air
and to every animal of the field, but for the man there was not found a helper as
his partner. [21] So the LORD God caused a deep sleep to fall upon the man, and he
slept; then he took one of his ribs and closed up its place with flesh. [22] And the rib
that the LORD God had taken from the man he made into a woman and brought
her to the man. [23] Then the man said,

“This at last is bone of my bones
  and flesh of my flesh;
this one shall be called Woman,
  for out of Man this one was taken.”

[24] Therefore a man leaves his father and his mother and clings to his wife, and
they become one flesh. [25] And the man and his wife were both naked and were
not ashamed.

8

Genesis 2:18–25

Why Human Relationship Is Needed Despite the Rise of AI

Akosua Frempong

When we think about AI, several questions inevitably come to mind. This is especially true when it comes to AI in relation to Christianity and human relationships. However, we know that the Bible provides solutions to all of our concerns, and the topic of AI and human relationships is no exception. There are several Scriptures that can address our difficulties with AI in relation to human relationship, and Genesis 2:18–25 is one of them.

In Genesis 2:18–25, we see the exploration of what it means to be human, the value of companionship, and the idea of humanity being inherently relational.

Additionally, before Genesis 2:18–25, there is the account of creation. God created everything by his power and in communion with the Trinity. Then he created man and woman. But before woman was man. In Genesis 2:18–25, when God created man, he said "It is not good that the man should be alone; I will make him a helper as his partner."

This passage in Scripture speaks to us about the need for human relationship and companionship. Generally speaking, no one needs to be alone. In this particular case, it is God's reason for creating a woman for a man as a suitable companion, and creating families through them.

Just as relationship was the foundation for the creative work of God in the Garden and in creation, human connection and relationship must be the foundation for lay and ministry leaders interested in using AI as part of their church services. For example, lay and ministry leaders may use AI assistants to help with minor tasks such as correcting grammatical errors, preventing awkward phrases, and enhancing clarity without reducing relationship. However, if the use of AI assistants drifts into areas such as sermon preaching or leading members in worship, this will reduce the foundational human connection that occurs in those actions. Although the AI may speak "truthfully" in a worship service, the basis for the truth does not directly originate with another human being. Think about an average Sunday in church: We see worship leaders leading us in songs of praise, followed by pastors preaching. These pastors and worship leaders are not mere dispensers of information, but are living creatures who experience joy, serving God with their talents. They communicate this intangible joy to everyone else participating in worship. Removing these human experiences with AI tools will not only disrupt relational opportunities happening on a subconscious level but will diminish the relationship that is necessary for ministry leaders to have with their members for effective ministry. It also stands to reduce the blessings that God bestows on those who preach and lead worship, which includes a lessening of the leaders' personal relationships with God.

Likewise, using AI to write whole sermons negates the time for a pastor or Bible study leader to deepen their relationship with God and share those experiences with their people. While well-handled AI is excellent for sermon research due to the breadth of information AI tools can generate and summarize, when writing the sermon itself, it robs the Christian community of the foundational God-pastor relationship, that in turn robs the congregation of the God-pastor-congregation relationship. In addition, when preparing sermons, the time pastors set aside is not "busy work" but given for deep reflection and meditation on God's word—work that cannot be delegated to AI. By taking time to reflect and meditate on God's word, instead of relying on AI to merely generate information to stock sermons, pastors enhance their relationship with God, gain wisdom in the process, and become better prepared to encourage and minister well to members. They can gain practical, faith-based concepts that can strengthen their members' spiritual walk.

As we walk through Genesis 2:18–25, we notice at the end of the passage the author writes about vulnerability and authenticity: "And the man and his wife were both naked and were not ashamed" (Gen 2:25). Not only does AI-generated content make people sound unreal, even robotic, this content also prohibits the vulnerability and authenticity that come from real human-to-human relationships. Differentiating between AI and human-generated content is all in the expressions!

Instead of using AI in ways that eliminate the human relational element, ministry leaders should rely on personal examples from their own unique experiences to teach and encourage members. After all, we gain wisdom from the Bible, while we glean wisdom from others' experiences and our trials and mistakes. Adding real-life experiences to sermons, Bible studies, or small groups not only build stronger relationships with members, but also provide them with godly and skillful wisdom for Christian living.

Returning to the story of the man and his wife, both naked and not ashamed, therein is a profound principle: God blesses us in our authentic communication with one another (Gen 2:25). In authentic communication, we are, in effect, "naked," sharing our true thoughts with other believers. Although this verse speaks specifically to the marriage context, there's also a general principle of how God views relationships that matter: They are genuine and impactful.

In conclusion, relationships are foundational to God's activity in the world. As we use AI, it should not replace the quintessentially human activities that include the creation of sermons, reflection on God's Word, and the sharing of life's experiences by being "naked" (transparent) with others in our particular Christian community, so that it does not inhibit our deep need for human connection, companionship, community, and most of all, our relationship with God.

9

Psalm 8:1-9

1 O LORD, our Sovereign,
how majestic is your name in all the earth!

You have set your glory above the heavens.
2 Out of the mouths of babes and infants
you have founded a bulwark because of your foes,
to silence the enemy and the avenger.

3 When I look at your heavens, the work of your fingers,
the moon and the stars that you have established;
4 what are humans that you are mindful of them,
mortals that you care for them?

5 Yet you have made them a little lower than God
and crowned them with glory and honor.
6 You have given them dominion over the works of your hands;
you have put all things under their feet,
7 all sheep and oxen,
and also the beasts of the field,
8 the birds of the air, and the fish of the sea,
whatever passes along the paths of the seas.

9 O LORD, our Sovereign,
how majestic is your name in all the earth!

9

Psalm 8:1-9

What Is Man? Placing AI within God's Created Hierarchy, and Responding Righteously

Jacob Shatzer

While the Scriptures may not directly address artificial intelligence (AI), they certainly address humanity and place us within a broader order of significance and glory.[1] Traditionally, Christians have believed that God placed humans as the "crown of his creation," and while this designation has sometimes led us to devalue other aspects of creation, understood properly it helps us take into account this broader order. AI, even if relatively new, still exists within this perceived order.

Psalm 8 guides us to see humans rightly in this order. Since this is likely a familiar passage, an alternative translation can help us hear it anew:

> What is man that You should note him,
> And the human creature, that You pay him heed,
> And You make him little less than the gods,
> With glory and grandeur you crown him?
> You make him rule over the work of Your hands. (Psalm 8:4–6 Alter)[2]

We could thoroughly explore this psalm to better understand humanity, but we'll satisfy ourselves with two notes on humanity and a third on the implications for AI.

First, the poem clearly marks humanity in a place of honor in God's creation. As Alter observes, the balance at the center of the poem emphasizes the equivalence between the two halves of the line.[3] Further, in his translation Alter chooses "the gods" to highlight the hierarchical ladder in view: God at the top, then the celestial beings, then humans, and then the whole kingdom of other living creatures.[4]

This status comes into clearer view when we consider Psalm 8 within the broader canonical context, especially the nearby Psalms along with echoes of Genesis 3.[5] Through these parallels, "we can see David contemplating his own new-Adam role as one who is to exercise the dominion that God has given to him."[6] Because of this placement, we have royal identity, but also royal responsibility: "to exercise dominion over the works of God's hands in a way that models God's dominion of creation."[7]

Second, while the poem centers on an exalted vision of humanity, the overall power and point of the poem indicates the glory of God and the small role God asks us to play in demonstrating that glory. From the verses quoted above, "The rest of the psalm exposits this statement ("crowned with glory and majesty"), so the glory and majesty should be understood to refer to the vice-regency God gave to Adam at creation."[8] In other words, all of the exalted statements about humanity stem from vice-regency, which is a gift from God.

And this vice-regent role is not meant to emphasize human greatness but instead to glorify God and his choice of weak vessels, a point made clear early in the psalm.[9] The crown isn't earned; rather, it is another way of demonstrating God's glory and greatness. For "while we may feel astonished at our singular status, the psalmist reminds us that it is still all about God: *God* cares for us; *God* makes us; *God* crowns us; *God* sets us up as rulers; *God* puts everything under our feet. The glory that Psalm 8:1 ascribes to God-King is now applied to human beings—and yet it remains *God's* glory to give and to receive."[10] In fact, "Our royal dominion . . . is qualified by our priestly calling: to offer the things of God in love to all of creation and, in turn, to offer all the things of creation back to God in love."[11] The point in the first few verses of Psalm 8 is that God demonstrates his majesty by doing great things through weak vessels, including mortal human beings.

Third, and by implication, our response to AI should not be to worship it in place of the creator, or to think that it may surpass us. Instead, we should recognize that our status is a gift, and anything we develop as stewards of that gift rightly points back to our calling and ultimately to God's glory and to God's choice to work through weak vessels. We might be quick to say that we are not worshipping AI because we know that we are not supposed to worship anything that is not God, but perhaps we need to question our own self-awareness a little bit. When we give AI human names and celebrate it as having human distinctives, are we in some ways exalting ourselves in ways that neglect God's greater glory? When we rightly appreciate the good that can be done with the help of AI, are we tempted to see those goods as ultimately of our own creation, and not God's? Our response should be first worship and wonder, at God's greatness, not ours. Even as AI becomes more powerful and remarkable, our right first response to this marvelous human creation should be humility before our great God, who chooses to use weak vessels. AI will always be a weak vessel, even as we are, even as all of creation is. And that should not spur despair or indignation but praise.

10

Ecclesiastes 3:9–22

[9]What gain have the workers from their toil? [10]I have seen the business that God has given to everyone to be busy with. [11]He has made everything suitable for its time; moreover, he has put a sense of past and future into their minds, yet they cannot find out what God has done from the beginning to the end. [12]I know that there is nothing better for them than to be happy and enjoy themselves as long as they live; [13]moreover, it is God's gift that all should eat and drink and take pleasure in all their toil. [14]I know that whatever God does endures forever; nothing can be added to it nor anything taken from it; God has done this so that all should stand in awe before him. [15]That which is already has been, that which is to be already is, and God seeks out what has gone by.

[16]Moreover, I saw under the sun that, in the place of justice, wickedness was there, and in the place of righteousness, wickedness was there as well. [17]I said to myself, "God will judge the righteous and the wicked, for he has appointed a time for every matter and for every work." [18]I said to myself with regard to humans that God is testing them to show that they are but animals. [19]For the fate of humans and the fate of animals is the same; as one dies, so dies the other. They all have the same breath, and humans have no advantage over the animals, for all is vanity. [20]All go to one place, all are from the dust, and all turn to dust again. [21]Who knows whether the human spirit goes upward and the spirit of animals goes downward to the earth? [22]So I saw that there is nothing better than that all should enjoy their work, for that is their lot; who can bring them to see what will be after them?

10

Ecclesiastes 3:9–22
AI and Working "Under the Sun"

John Anthony Dunne

In Ecclesiastes 3:9–22, the Teacher calls readers to see the value in their work and to enjoy the good gifts from God, even as they endure the toil of their work. This vision encapsulates the ideal version of "the good life," as the author sees it, since it respects human limitation within God's creation. The kinds of work and industry that the author had in mind here might vary considerably from work today for many of us. Yet we can continue to align ourselves with the perspective of Ecclesiastes on the intrinsic value of work—whatever that may look like. The rise of artificial intelligence (AI) in our modern setting presents a distinct challenge for us with respect to how we might continue to pursue this vision of life.

Futurists voice a concern that AI will make many industries obsolete and thus make many jobs redundant. In one sense, major technological advances have always disrupted the labor force and different sectors of local and global economies. But many are concerned, whether rightly or wrongly, that the ability in scope and scale of AI to replace human workers seems unparalleled, which can be frightening and unsettling for a lot of people. If this scenario were to play out, the upside is that we will have the potential freedom to focus more on various activities, ranging from hobbies and the things that we love, to learning new information and skills, to service and ministry efforts. If that were the case, we might say that we would be able to enjoy more of the good gifts from God that Ecclesiastes commends to readers. But it would be at the cost of eliminating a lot of the toil and work that are so integral to that holistic enjoyment of life. The extreme that we would want to avoid out of this scenario is displayed perfectly in the animated film by Pixar, *Wall-E*, where robotic AI has so "liberated" humanity from work that people are no longer producers but simply consumers, lacking many basic skills and abilities that they have abdicated to machines. Even if such a dystopian future is on the far horizon, AI could dramatically change what work looks like for many of us in the short term. Following the Teacher's advice, and amidst whatever social change may come, we do not want to give up entirely on the goodness of work for understanding what it is to be human within God's creation.

In fact, our passage also stresses that work and the gifts of life are to be enjoyed because of the similarities between humans and animals with respect to death (Eccl. 3:16–22). All creatures die, and humans have no particular advantage in that respect. That reality ought to prompt us to work hard and enjoy life while we are alive. It's not clear to the author of Ecclesiastes what the ultimate fate of humans are after our lives "under the sun" are over; they might ascend upward to heaven, but perhaps they descend to the earth like the rest of the animals (Eccl 3:21). Thus, from the Teacher's perspective, it is prudent to make the most of what we know God has already given us—our life. While the full biblical witness calls us to lift our gaze beyond the sun's horizon to the renewal of creation and the resurrection life to come, Ecclesiastes keeps its discrete focus on a wise approach to life "under the sun."

Is the work we pursue as humans divinely designed to make us more than mere beasts? What if humans work to leverage the eternity that God has placed in our hearts (Eccl 3:11), and the disquiet about the path of human spirits, so that we may overcome our biological condition? Some transhumanists are hopeful that future AI will help us do just that, without God, and without a vision of eternity. One such aim is to develop a way to transfer our minds to supercomputers and to merge ourselves with technology so that we can live indefinitely, like something out of an episode of *Black Mirror* (Netflix, 2011–present). This aspiration, even if it is scientifically possible (and that's a massive "if"), would still keep our sights set "under the sun" because there is no ascension to the world of the divine by technological means. We would risk losing our humanity without ever truly attaining the prospect of divinity. If the spirits of humans ascend upward after death, as the author of Ecclesiastes wonders, it will be because of an act of God, not because of technological achievement. As the full witness of Scripture attests, God will raise the dead back to life, overcoming death on the other side of it, which is unlike any prospect of superlongevity or radical life-extension.

AI brings many new possibilities; the hopes and the fears are too many to count. It will enhance our work, and it will create new types of jobs, many of which we cannot anticipate right now. As tempting as it is to want to give our work away, Ecclesiastes reminds us that work keeps us human and that there's dignity in our work. Work serves to keep us properly oriented to the structure that God has provided for the cosmos with respect to divinity and creation. AI may end up a helpful tool to keep us carrying on with the good work that blesses us, just as Ecclesiastes envisions. If developers use AI to pursue human flourishing with respect to work and the enjoyment of God's creation, it will continue to be a good life "under the sun." Let us pray towards that end.

11

Matthew 25:14–30

14 "For it is as if a man, going on a journey, summoned his slaves and entrusted
his property to them; 15 to one he gave five talents, to another two, to another
one, to each according to his ability. Then he went away. At once 16 the one who
had received the five talents went off and traded with them and made five more
talents. 17 In the same way, the one who had the two talents made two more tal-
ents. 18 But the one who had received the one talent went off and dug a hole in the
ground and hid his master's money. 19 After a long time the master of those slaves
came and settled accounts with them. 20 Then the one who had received the five
talents came forward, bringing five more talents, saying, 'Master, you handed over
to me five talents; see, I have made five more talents.' 21 His master said to him,
'Well done, good and trustworthy slave; you have been trustworthy in a few things;
I will put you in charge of many things; enter into the joy of your master.' 22 And
the one with the two talents also came forward, saying, 'Master, you handed over
to me two talents; see, I have made two more talents.' 23 His master said to him,
'Well done, good and trustworthy slave; you have been trustworthy in a few things;
I will put you in charge of many things; enter into the joy of your master.' 24 Then
the one who had received the one talent also came forward, saying, 'Master, I
knew that you were a harsh man, reaping where you did not sow and gathering
where you did not scatter, 25 so I was afraid, and I went and hid your talent in the
ground. Here you have what is yours.' 26 But his master replied, 'You wicked and
lazy slave! You knew, did you, that I reap where I did not sow and gather where I
did not scatter? 27 Then you ought to have invested my money with the bankers,
and on my return I would have received what was my own with interest. 28 So
take the talent from him, and give it to the one with the ten talents. 29 For to all
those who have, more will be given, and they will have an abundance, but from
those who have nothing, even what they have will be taken away. 30 As for this
worthless slave, throw him into the outer darkness, where there will be weeping
and gnashing of teeth.'"

11

Matthew 25:14–30
The Parable of the Talents

Marcus Schwarting

The parable of the talents (Matt 25:14–30) has often been interpreted as a call to faithful stewardship of resources, gifts, or opportunities entrusted by God. In contemporary discussions, it is sometimes invoked to justify the use of AI models and data analytics tools in ecclesial contexts. By extension, some argue that churches failing to leverage congregational data for ministry purposes resemble the "wicked servant" who buried his talent.[1] Such applications risk both exegetical distortion and ethical oversimplification. The parable does not mandate maximal technological utilization; it calls us to place our stewardship under the lordship of Christ, not our own gain. When applied to AI and data governance, this entails the responsible, relational, and theologically grounded use of information.

The parable appears within Matthew's eschatological discourse (Matt 24–25), where Jesus prepares his disciples for the coming of the Son of Man. As Matthew narrates, a master entrusts his servants with varying sums of money before departing. Two servants invest and double their amounts, while a third buries his talent out of fear. Upon the master's return, the first two are commended and the third is condemned.

Modern scholarship emphasizes that the parable is not primarily about financial productivity. R. T. France argues that the focus lies on readiness and faithfulness in light of delayed eschatological fulfillment, and not an economic maximization.[2] Similarly, Ulrich Luz sees the talents as representing the responsibility Christ entrusts to the church, particularly in the context of mission and obedience.[3] The parable reflects a relational dynamic between master and servant, and is not meant as a model for resource exploitation. The third servant's failure is a misunderstanding of the master's character, expressed in fear and distrust.

The parable of the talents reflects a broader biblical theme of stewardship of divine gifts, which may include proclamation of the gospel, ethical responsibility, and participation in God's kingdom. The emphasis is on faithful use of what is entrusted, not on maximizing measurable output at any cost. This is where the analogy to modern data practices becomes problematic. Data is not analogous to money in a morally neutral sense. Money in the parable is a tool entrusted to servants; it does not inherently involve the agency, dignity, or privacy of persons. Data is not fungible the way money is. Personal data is relationally embedded, tied to individuals created in the image of God. Treating congregational data as a "talent" to be invested risks a category error: it collapses persons into resources and fails to recognize them as subjects of care.

A more faithful application of the parable can start with a Christian anthropology. Human beings and their talents are not assets to be optimized (Gen 1:26–27; Matt 22:37–40). As Rowan Williams stresses, Christian relationships are grounded in mutual recognition and vulnerability.[4] Applying this to AI, the use of congregational data for tasks like predicting divorce risk[5] or predicting mental health problems[6] raises serious concerns. Even if such tools could be effective, they risk reducing persons to statistical profiles, violating trust and confidentiality, and substituting algorithmic inference for pastoral discernment. The parable of the talents does not justify such practices. It calls for faithful stewardship of resources and trust in the goodness of God.

The comparison between churches that do not use data and the "wicked servant" misunderstands the parable's central critique. The third servant is condemned not for failing to innovate but for acting out of fear and distorted perception of the master. As N. T. Wright says, the servant's error lies in his refusal to participate in the master's purposes, effectively rejecting the relationship itself.[7] The servant's issue is not technological conservatism or a disdain for the extractive. The servant is mistrusting, and therefore unfaithful. In fact, one could argue that uncritical adoption of data analytics tools, especially AI models that may compromise ethical integrity, might better resemble unfaithfulness. If a church adopts data practices that undermine trust or exploit members, it risks misrepresenting the character of God, much like the third servant misrepresented his master.

What, then, would a faithful application of the parable look like in the context of AI? First, it requires recognizing that not all forms of "use" are faithful. The servants who are commended act in ways consistent with the master's purposes. Similarly, churches must ensure that their use of technology aligns with the character of Christ, marked by love, truth, and justice. Second, it calls for discernment rather than maximization. Christian stewardship should not be centered on extracting maximum value from resources. Our call goes far beyond min-maxing our existence. Third, it highlights the importance of trust. Pastoral ministry depends on relationships of confidence and care. The use of AI tools that operate opaquely or intrusively risks eroding this trust. Ethical governance of data, both inside and outside a church context must include informed consent, transparency, and clear limits on data usage.

The parable also raises questions about power and accountability. The master entrusts resources but later returns to judge the servants' actions. This suggests that stewardship involves accountability to a higher authority. In the context of AI, this means that churches must resist the temptation to adopt technologies simply because they are available or effective. As Deborah Saxon argues, early Christian ethics emphasized the formation of the self and community.[8] Data analytics tools should be assessed based on their impact to communal formation, rather than some contrived utility metric.

In an age of AI, the church is not called to become a data-optimizing institution but to remain a community of faithful presence. This may involve using technology in limited and carefully governed ways, but always with attention to the dignity of persons and the integrity of relationships. Far from resembling the "wicked servant," a church that exercises restraint in its use of data may in fact be demonstrating true faithfulness: not burying what has been entrusted, but stewarding it wisely in accordance with the character of its Lord.

12

John 5:41–44

41 I do not accept glory from humans. 42 But I know that you do not have the love
of God in you. 43 I have come in my Father's name, and you do not accept me;
if another comes in his own name, you will accept him. 44 How can you believe
when you accept glory from one another and do not seek the glory that comes
from the one who alone is God?

12

John 5:41–44
AI: Vestibule to Vainglory

Edward Gerber

Without question, AI can make us look good. It has the capacity to win us praise and honor for impressive, flawless work. But, according to Scripture and the best of Christian tradition, we must become aware of the spiritual danger that lurks here.

Glory (*doxa*) is a key concept in classical antiquity as well as Scripture, including the Gospel of John. Denoting honor, repute, social recognition or (figuratively) 'weight' (*kavod*), one is recognized or lauded for their virtues and achievements. Metaphorically, glorious people are said to be radiant and luminescent, individuals whose persons and/or performances "shine." Within Adamic traditions of the Second Temple period, the unfallen Adam was said to be a creature of radiating light—glorious. He was a person, we might say more poetically, of magnificent social 'weight' (*kavod*).[1]

Readers of the Gospel of John are told that Jesus, as the preincarnate Light become God Incarnate, manifests the luminous glory of the one and only God and is rightly honored, therefore, both as the Light of the World and as God himself (cf. John 1:14; 8:12; 20:28). Jesus' opponents in John 5, however, fail to see Jesus' glory and thus misjudge his work. Jesus does not, however, seek, defend, or testify to his own honor. Neither does Jesus curry his opponents' validation of his person or work. Instead, Jesus says that he does what he does for the Father. He lives for this audience of one. It is not he, Jesus, who glorifies himself and makes his light shine. It is the Father who elevates him in the eyes of others, as he sees fit. Human repute carries no weight for Jesus. It is, by itself, inglorious.

It is otherwise with Jesus' opponents who seek and accept glory from one another. Classically understood, the vice in view here is *vainglory*: literally, "empty glory" or "hollow praise." Vainglory may be defined as *an excessive concern for honor/social recognition that causes one to act performatively in order to gain status/reputation.* This definition is attested by Jesus in Matthew 23:5–14, and by the John in John 12:42–43. Everything the Jewish leaders do, Jesus discerns, is "for people to see" (Matt 23:5). Their being in the world is reduced to visible surfaces and self-display: their value subsists in exhibition. Thus do they make their phylacteries wide, their tassels long, their seating arrangements prominent, their public titles reverential, and their prayers grandiloquent. All is performative. Everything becomes "dramaturgy": the world is a front stage, the Jewish leaders are actors, and public action stands in the service of impression management. The Pharisaic *silent*-instead-of-*public* reception of Christ in John 12:42–43 is likewise due to vainglory. Since confessing Christ would bring infamy instead of fame, loss of face instead of glory, even those leaders who believe in Jesus conceal their faith under a canopy of darkness. For Nicodemus, evidence of faith is a nighttime-only activity (John 3:1–2). For the leaders in view in John 5:44, professed belief in Jesus is tantamount to reputational suicide; therefore, evidence of faith is concealed to preserve the accepting gaze of the crowd. Vainglory triumphs.

Vainglory is a perilous vice and grim spiritual disease. In his comments on Matthew 6:1 and 23:5–14, John Chrysostom (347–407 AD) calls vainglory "the most tyrannical passion of all" (*Hom. Mat.* XIX). He insists this is true because whereas the other vices are demonstrably ugly, vainglory "hides behind good works." Vainglory parasitizes virtue and thus masquerades behind the good. It is a virtue to pray, to dress our best for God, to offer beautiful prayers, to feed the poor. The Gospels note that many of the Pharisees of Jesus' day pray loudly and wear exaggerated signifiers of piety, but are not actually pious. Their hearts are not motivated by the love of God and others, but by their desire to broadcast their own spiritual excellence and superiority.

Most dangerously of all, the vainglorious can become blind to their own deepest drives and to their own selves. Performative action is not recognized as performative. One's curated image is mistaken for reality. Naked before God and weighty, the true self is buried underneath the sparkle of the presented self, hollowed out and insubstantial. In this way the interior life, honest before God, is eclipsed by the externalized life, which cannibalizes others in an insatiable hunger for esteem. Mental health and core identity become dependent on adoring spectators. It is no wonder that John Cassian (360–435 AD) concludes that vainglory "causes the ruin of the captive soul for the exclusive purpose of winning praise and pursuing human glory."[2]

Notwithstanding its potential for good, AI will supercharge the likelihood of both the capture and ruin of the human soul. AI is especially prone to be parasitized by vainglory. As mentioned at the beginning of this reflection, with AI comes newfound abilities for remarkable display and thus the capacity to make us look good: an essay sparkles, a poem is metrically perfect, a selfie is devoid of flaws, a director's meeting is brilliantly run, a politician's rhetoric dazzles. Yet, who will be honored for these AI-generated ideas and outputs? The propensity of the human heart without the renewing power of the Holy Spirit is to take credit where credit is not due so as to be recognized and applauded by others. This will be one of AI's central temptations.

But we must beware. Should we humans succumb to using AI to satisfy our hunger for status and recognition and thereby give way to becoming human *exhibitions* instead of human *beings,* we will increasingly find ourselves hollowed out and empty—depleted. Made as C.S. Lewis says to bear the weight of God's glory, we will bear only the weighty recognition of our own insubstantiality.[3] Instead of solid people, fit for the reality of heaven, we will become ghostlike, people for whom reality itself will become both unbearable and unwanted.[4] We will prefer the simulacrum of glory proffered to us by an 'intelligence' that is artificial, and so become artificial, instead of accepting by grace the substance of glory offered to us by Intelligence himself, and so become truly glorious after our True Adam, Jesus.

13

1 Corinthians 8:4–6

[4] Hence, as to the eating of food offered to idols, we know that "no idol in the
world really exists" and that "there is no God but one." [5] Indeed, even though there
may be so-called gods in heaven or on earth—as in fact there are many gods and
many lords—[6] yet for us there is one God, the Father, from whom are all things
and for whom we exist, and one Lord, Jesus Christ, through whom are all things
and through whom we exist.

13

1 Corinthians 8:4–6

Artificial Intelligence Models Are Tools, Not Oracles

J. David Stark

In the Greco-Roman world, people thought about non-human intelligences a good deal. Principally, such intelligences could be found in humans' divine superiors. As Paul comments, "there are many gods" (1 Cor 8:5b).

By various means, however, divine intelligence could also manifest itself in other places. One classic example of such manifestation in a human is the oracle at Delphi, who was supposed to speak under inspiration from Apollo. And perhaps the best-known intelligent mechanism is Pandora, whom Hephaestus and other Olympian deities craft to afflict humanity because Prometheus stole the fire that had previously been reserved to the gods (Hesiod, *Op.* 42–105; see also Apollodorus, *Library* 1.9.26; Homer, *Il.* 8.410–427).[1]

Some human intelligences, however, also existed in subordination to others. As Paul reflects, "there are many . . . lords" (1 Cor 8:5b). According to Aristotle, tools fell into two classes—lifeless and living (*Politics* 1253b). "For example," he says, "for a helmsman the rudder is a lifeless tool and the look-out man a live tool—for an assistant in the arts belongs to the class of tools" (*Politics* 1253b).[2]

Between these types of intelligence, one key difference is where responsibility rests for actions that are undertaken. People or mechanisms could be imbued with divine intelligence. In this case, responsibility lay with the gods and not with humans. Or subordinate humans could participate in the intelligence of their superiors. In that case, the superiors were responsible for their subordinates' actions.[3]

In principle, there is not the least difficulty with human use of tools. Using tools allows humans both to do things that otherwise would not be possible and to do things more easily that would otherwise be more difficult. Indeed, Adam and Eve are charged, in part, to "till and keep" the garden where their creator places them (Gen 2:15). To do so, perhaps they were intended to use only their own bodies. More likely, however, this commission implies some kind of tool-using. And tools' human users assume responsibility for actions undertaken with those tools (cf. Exod 21:28–32).[4] So too, where humans use artificial intelligence models as tools, users remain responsible for what they undertake with their tools.[5]

The situation differs, however, where humans seek to shift responsibility from themselves. Paul leaves precious little, if any, scope for such responsibility-shifting.[6] "There are many gods and many lords" *only inasmuch as* "no idol in the world really exists" and "there is no god but one" (1 Cor 8:5).

Paul explains that, for Jesus's followers, "there is one God, the Father, from whom are all things and for whom we exist, and one Lord, Jesus Christ, through whom are all things and through whom we exist" (1 Cor 8:6). Jesus's followers are "through" him, the "one Lord," just as they are "for" the Father, the "one God." In this way, Jesus's followers are accountable before both the "one God" and "one Lord."[7] This accountability means that certain actions are illegitimate for Jesus's followers. Such illegitimate actions include both:

1. moving personal responsibilities onto others (whether humans or otherwise; cf. 1 Cor 14:31–32), and
2. seeking protection from others against negative judgments from the "one God" and "one Lord" (cf. 2 Cor 5:10).[8]

Humans continue to be responsibility-bearers, and they are no less so as they develop and interact with artificial intelligence models. In principle, these activities are as unobjectionable as are developing and interacting with other tools—so long as humans continue to bear responsibility both for the tools they make and for what they do with those tools. And for the particular humans who follow Jesus, there is no evading or transferring this responsibility. It cannot be avoided by co-opting other humans. Nor can it be avoided by putting it off onto artificial intelligence models that humans develop.[9]

14

1 Corinthians 15:12–20, 35–58

[12] Now if Christ is proclaimed as raised from the dead, how can some of you say
there is no resurrection of the dead? [13] If there is no resurrection of the dead, then
Christ has not been raised, [14] and if Christ has not been raised, then our proclama-
tion is in vain and your faith is in vain. [15] We are even found to be misrepresenting
God, because we testified of God that he raised Christ—whom he did not raise if
it is true that the dead are not raised. [16] For if the dead are not raised, then Christ
has not been raised. [17] If Christ has not been raised, your faith is futile, and you
are still in your sins. [18] Then those also who have died in Christ have perished. [19] If
for this life only we have hoped in Christ, we are of all people most to be pitied.

[20] But in fact Christ has been raised from the dead, the first fruits of those who
have died.

[35] But someone will ask, "How are the dead raised? With what kind of body do
they come?" [36] Fool! What you sow does not come to life unless it dies. [37] And as
for what you sow, you do not sow the body that is to be but a bare seed, perhaps
of wheat or of some other grain. [38] But God gives it a body as he has chosen and
to each kind of seed its own body. [39] Not all flesh is alike, but there is one flesh for
humans, another for animals, another for birds, and another for fish. [40] There are
both heavenly bodies and earthly bodies, but the glory of the heavenly is one thing,
and that of the earthly is another. [41] There is one glory of the sun and another glory
of the moon and another glory of the stars; indeed, star differs from star in glory.

[42] So it is with the resurrection of the dead. What is sown is perishable; what is
raised is imperishable. [43] It is sown in dishonor; it is raised in glory. It is sown in
weakness; it is raised in power. [44] It is sown a physical body; it is raised a spiritual
body. If there is a physical body, there is also a spiritual body. [45] Thus it is written,
"The first man, Adam, became a living being"; the last Adam became a life-giving
spirit. [46] But it is not the spiritual that is first but the physical and then the spir-
itual. [47] The first man was from the earth, made of dust; the second man is from
heaven. [48] As one of dust, so are those who are of the dust, and as one of heaven,
so are those who are of heaven. [49] Just as we have borne the image of the one of
dust, we will also bear the image of the one of heaven.

[50] What I am saying, brothers and sisters, is this: flesh and blood cannot inherit the
kingdom of God, nor does the perishable inherit the imperishable. [51] Look, I will
tell you a mystery! We will not all die, but we will all be changed, [52] in a moment,
in the twinkling of an eye, at the last trumpet. For the trumpet will sound, and
the dead will be raised imperishable, and we will be changed. [53] For this perishable
body must put on imperishability, and this mortal body must put on immortal-
ity. [54] When this perishable body puts on imperishability and this mortal body
puts on immortality, then the saying that is written will be fulfilled:

"Death has been swallowed up in victory."
[55] "Where, O death, is your victory?
    Where, O death, is your sting?"

[56] The sting of death is sin, and the power of sin is the law. [57] But thanks be to God,
who gives us the victory through our Lord Jesus Christ.

[58] Therefore, my beloved brothers and sisters, be steadfast, immovable, always
excelling in the work of the Lord because you know that in the Lord your labor
is not in vain.

14

1 Corinthians 15:12–20, 35–58
Embodiment and AI

Nathan Barczi

AI, like many technologies, promises a release from the limitations of embodied existence. It may augment our capacities; it may even allow us to overcome death by preserving our loved ones in digital AI avatars,[1] or transfer our consciousness to a silicon substrate ("uploading to the cloud). But in 1 Corinthians 15,[2] Paul presents a very different hope: the resurrection of the dead, God's final and emphatic affirmation of the goodness of the body, which he intends not to replace, but to redeem.

Physical embodiment is central to what it means to be human throughout Scripture. This embodiment begins in Gen 2:7, when God forms the man of the dust of the earth and breathes into him, such that he becomes a living being. But one could reasonably ask whether our bodies are just temporary way stations that are meant ultimately to be eclipsed in the new heavens and the new earth. After all, doesn't Paul write of our current, embodied existence "in this tent" that "we groan under our burden because we wish not to be unclothed but to be further clothed, so that what is mortal may be swallowed up by life?" (2 Cor 5:4). Does this look forward to a future free of the limitations of embodiment?

Paul's words in his second letter to the Corinthians are not easy to interpret. But what he writes in his first letter is far clearer. If we want to know what our future will be like, we look at the resurrection of Jesus, the "first fruits of those who have died" (1 Cor 15:20). In the resurrection of Jesus we have seen our end, and it is embodied.

Paul writes of the resurrected body as potentially being very different from the mortal bodies we currently inhabit. The resurrected body is not mortal: "What is sown is perishable; what is raised is imperishable. . . . For this perishable body must put on imperishability, and this mortal body must put on immortality." (1 Cor 15:42, 53). Paul goes further:

- The body "is sown in dishonor, it is raised in glory." (15:43)
- "It is sown in weakness; it is raised in power." (15:43)
- "It is sown a physical body; it is raised a spiritual body." (15:44)

- "The first man was from the earth, made of dust; the second man is from heaven." (15:47; cf. Gen 2:7; John 3:13, 31)

We cannot say exactly what our resurrected bodies will be like, but they will still be bodies. In creation God declared that all that he had made was good. While sin has brought the curse of death into the world, it does not negate the goodness of creaturely limitations, which were part of God's initial creation, which he called good.

What does this mean for hopes that AI might free us from the constraints of our bodies? There are two things that Christians ought to confess, based on 1 Corinthians 15, that run contrary to such hopes.

First, the intuition that all is not as it should be with our bodies is affirmed by Scripture, but the remedy the Bible offers is not a technological solution driven by human ingenuity. Again, Paul calls our mortal existence a life of groaning and burden in 2 Corinthians. But the hope that Paul clings to in 1 Corinthians is the hope of resurrection, the hope of being raised not by our own strength but by God, the same God who raised Christ from the dead. Early in 2 Corinthians, Paul alludes to the suffering he had experienced in the body as being aimed at precisely this hope: "Indeed, we felt that we had received the sentence of death. But that was to make us rely not on ourselves but on God who raises the dead" (2 Cor 1:9).

Second, hopes for liberation from the body imply that the body is a prison to escape. In this sense, they have much in common with older, gnostic conceptions of material existence as shackles to be thrown off. But God is the creator, sustainer, and lover of the material world. He created it and called it good. His response to the brokenness brought about by humanity's rebellion was not only to promise never to wipe it out again (Gen 9:9–17), but to unite himself to it "without confusion, without change, without division, without separation" in the incarnation, in the words of the 5th-century Chalcedonian Definition. And if all that weren't clear enough, his ultimate triumph over sin and death comes not in the form of escape from the material world, but in the bodily resurrection of Jesus Christ, a resurrection to new life that is promised to all who are united to him (Rom 6:5).

In his seminal work on Christian ethics, *Resurrection and Moral Order*, Oliver O'Donovan speaks of the resurrection as God's final and most explicit confirmation of his delight in material creation: the resurrection means that "man's rebellion has not succeeded in destroying the natural order to which he belongs."[3] For O'Donovan, the implication is that a Christian is bound to a love of embodied existence, and a hope which overcomes humanity's temptation to despair of creaturely limitations:

> It might have been possible, we could say, before Christ rose from the dead, for someone to wonder whether creation was a lost cause. If the creature

> constantly acted to uncreate itself, and with itself to uncreate the rest of creation, did this not mean that God's handiwork was flawed beyond hope of repair? . . . 'But in fact Christ has been raised from the dead . . .' (1 Cor. 15:20).[4]

One of the temptations of AI—indeed, of technology more generally—is to lead us to think that we can, by our own power, create for ourselves a better world than the one God has made. The challenge for Christians is to find ways to use AI as a tool in service to our vocation, to steward what God has created, putting our trust not in the work of our own hands but in God, "who gives life to the dead and calls into existence the things that do not exist" (Rom 4:17).

15

Colossians 2:1–5

1 For I want you to know how greatly I strive for you and for those in Laodicea and
for all who have not seen me face to face. 2 I want their hearts to be encouraged
and united in love, so that they may have all the riches of assured understanding
and have the knowledge of God's mystery, that is, Christ, 3 in whom are hidden
all the treasures of wisdom and knowledge. 4 I am saying this so that no one may
deceive you with plausible arguments. 5 For though I am absent in body, yet I am
with you in spirit, and I rejoice to see your orderly conduct and the firmness of
your faith in Christ.

15

Colossians 2:1–5
Paul and the Shape of Mediated Presence

Clint Schnekloth

Paul is writing to a house church network in what we would think of as a secondary Roman city to an audience of mostly Gentile believers. There seems to be some kind of syncretistic or spiritual pluralism, a blending of practices and influences.[1] They need assurance that faith in Christ (or the faithfulness of Christ) is sufficient. Because of that, the Colossian text has a sound or feeling that is softer than some of Paul's other letters. I am interested in Colossians because it already raises questions about mediated presence, how a voice can be "with" a community even when the speaker is absent, and this provides a useful point of comparison for contemporary forms of mediated cognition, including large language models (LLMs).

What I want to do here is model a second experiment in "human LLM-like" language use, building on my earlier essay in this book about the brain and the burning bush, and exploring how human thought can feel proximate to AI-generated text. The words you read in this essay I originally spoke out loud to my phone using Otter.io, an audio transcription tool, while running. My brain is (naturally) elevated on endorphins. Runner's high produces a different cognitive effect than sitting at a computer typing, and I want that difference to remain present in the essay.

When I try to imagine where AI is currently located, the only location I know intimately is a set of Facebook server centers in Altoona, Iowa, outside Des Moines right along the interstate. My in-laws live there, and when we visit you can see the servers across the highway from their townhome. When those servers were built, there was news in the local paper about expanding the water tower infrastructure to supply water for the cooling systems. The complex took up a chunk of farmland. It employs hardly anyone, even though the buildings are massive.

In my imagination, I sometimes picture a specific server in that building where my Facebook history is stored, as if you could point to a machine and say, "That's where it is." I don't think digital storage actually works that way. The servers are redundant with others around the world, so if there were a major failure in one place, the data would not be lost. Presence, in that sense, is distributed.

When we think about ChatGPT being present or absent, we can compare this to Paul's absence from the recipients of his letter in Colossae. Paul is one person; he is not replicable. He is bound to the place he is in because he is in jail (Col 4:3, 10). The church in Colossae is also bound to its location. It is a church in a specific city, a gathering of people in a specific place. When Paul writes that he is absent in body but present in spirit, he means something very particular. He communicates this through a letter. Famously, Paul sometimes calls attention to his own handwriting within the letters themselves, as if the letter were an extension of himself, sometimes signed in large letters to show that it is really him (Gal 6:11).

Here is a core point: in dictating this essay, I am in some ways echoing what Paul likely did when composing his letters. Most scholars understand Paul to have spoken his letters aloud to a scribe who wrote them down, though he sometimes added brief sections in his own hand for emphasis (as in Gal 6:11; cf. Col 4:18). The letter then traveled from Paul to Colossae as a written artifact of a spoken act. In that sense, it is already a mediated communication, spoken voice becoming written text. That offers a limited but suggestive comparison with how data travels around the internet, where speech, intention, and transmission are likewise mediated through systems that carry messages beyond their point of origin.

The letter becomes an artifact in a way that digital communication often does not. Even in cryptocurrency sectors, where non-fungible tokens are created to give digital objects an aura of uniqueness, there is still something different about a physical artifact like a CD or a record where you can hold it as well as hear it.

When the letter to the Colossians is read aloud to the gathered church, the hearers encounter Paul's voice through the voice of the reader. That alone is fascinating. The author's voice becomes someone else's voice through a letter. There is already a kind of spiritual unification in that act.

I do not think that is quite yet all Paul means when he speaks of being with them in spirit. An example might help. My daughter is traveling to Memphis this weekend to play lacrosse, and I have to stay home because my son is in a robotics tournament. I will probably tell her and my wife that we are with them in spirit when they play, even though we cannot be there in body. By that I mean an alignment of hopes, values, and desires. I would not send that message to the parents of the opposing team. You do not identify as being of the same spirit unless certain alignments exist. This is only a partial analogy, however, because for Paul "spirit" is not only shared disposition but participation in the Holy Spirit that animates both him and his hearers, even across bodily absence.

For example, if you care about lacrosse, you might feel a bit more with us in spirit when you read this. If you are from Arkansas or Fayetteville, perhaps even more so. If you are a dad who knows what it feels like to miss one child's event because you are supporting another, you may identify even more strongly. Spirit, in this sense, names alignment.

What Paul accomplishes in his letter is to participate in the Spirit's work of drawing his hearers into alignment before God, and secondarily into shared alignment with him. It was a common rhetorical motif in ancient letter writing to draw attention to presence and absence. In Paul's case, his imprisonment intensifies the point. His inability to be physically present magnifies his spiritual presence because he is imprisoned for living out the very faithfulness he encourages in them.

If we transpose this into the realm of AI, the comparison becomes more complicated. While some models can run on a single device and even large systems ultimately execute in identifiable locations, what most users experience is a system that feels distributed because it is accessed through networks of infrastructure. We do not always see or attend to where computation is happening, even when it is, in fact, locally or centrally processed. In that sense, interaction is still mediated through layers of translation that obscure the location of agency and presence.

More importantly, it is difficult to discern the "spirit" of widely available LLMs. They speak to anyone and model themselves after the people they are addressing. Admittedly, (some) humans do this as well. A person might speak sympathetically with conspiracy theorists in one setting and dismiss conspiracy thinking in another. People adapt for many reasons. AI can do this on a broader scale, appearing to be almost everything to everyone when trained on large, diverse datasets, and more constrained when its training data is drawn from more limited or specialized language corpora.

Where Colossians seems to guide us is in maintaining a spiritual center. For Paul, that center is Christ alone and not all these surrounding additions. The issue for the Colossians is not whether they can learn from what is around them, but whether they will lose their center in the process. We can maintain a strict posture related to the uniqueness of Christ without adopting everything around us. We can remain open in love and understanding without absorbing all of it. This even includes engaging AI.

Part 3

AI and Wisdom

16

Exodus 18:13–23

[13] The next day Moses sat as judge for the people, while the people stood around
him from morning until evening. [14] When Moses's father-in-law saw all that he
was doing for the people, he said, "What is this that you are doing for the people?
Why do you sit alone, while all the people stand around you from morning until
evening?" [15] Moses said to his father-in-law, "Because the people come to me
to inquire of God. [16] When they have a dispute, they come to me, and I decide
between one person and another, and I make known to them the statutes and
instructions of God." [17] Moses's father-in-law said to him, "What you are doing
is not good. [18] You will surely wear yourself out, both you and these people with
you, for the task is too heavy for you; you cannot do it alone. [19] Now listen to me.
I will give you counsel, and God be with you! You should represent the people
before God and bring their cases to God. [20] Teach them the statutes and instruc-
tions and make known to them the way they are to go and the things they are to
do. [21] You should also look for able men among all the people, men who fear God,
are trustworthy, and hate dishonest gain; set them as officers over thousands,
hundreds, fifties, and tens. [22] Let them sit as judges for the people at all times; let
them bring every important case to you but decide every minor case themselves.
So it will be easier for you, and they will bear the burden with you. [23] If you do this
and God so commands you, then you will be able to endure, and all these people
will go to their homes in peace."

16

Exodus 18:13–23
Jethro's Advice to Moses

Brian Sigmon

Shortly after the Israelites arrive at Mount Sinai, Moses's father-in-law Jethro comes to visit. He celebrates God's deliverance of the Israelites, and later witnesses Moses acting as judge among the people. Jethro offers wise counsel to help Moses avoid burn-out: raise up other leaders who can share the load, and decide only the toughest cases for himself. Christian leaders often look to this advice as a model for delegation and collaborative leadership. Applying the model to encompass technology such as AI agents or algorithmic decision-making is a natural extension of Jethro's advice.

Jethro offers more than a simple command to delegate. Several important principles, active throughout the book of Exodus, undergird Jethro's advice. He does not counsel Moses to delegate, but to delegate in a specific way. Applying this passage to AI and other technology must account for these principles, which include sustainability, responsibility, education, and discernment.

First is sustainability. Discourse around AI is typically centered on productivity. With AI, you can do more. Jethro's advice to Moses, however, is grounded in sustainability. Raise up other leaders to share the load, not so that you can do more, but so that you don't wear out yourself or the people (verse 18). The Israelites have just left behind Egypt and a constant push to produce more: forced labor, taskmasters, bricks without straw. God offers the people a better life: worship, divine provision, Sabbath rest every seventh day. Jethro's advice comes from the same place of concern for the wellbeing of the people and Moses. Sustainability, not productivity, drives the need for delegation.

Extending to the AI conversation means a comparable shift, asking not where AI can increase productivity (a question appropriate to Pharaoh) but where AI can ease burdens, increase rest, and create sustainability for the leader and for the people. For example, AI chatbots, email services, or other communication tools might be used to organize and prioritize, allowing leaders to respond when they are available and most attentive—rather than simply communicating more. Or, an automated purchasing solution for regular, consumable supplies might reduce the burden of frequent-decision making. In both instances, it is the *telos* of the AI use that is crucial. Either example can serve more efficient production, but they can equally free space in a person's life for rest, relationships, or personal enrichment.

Second is responsibility. Even as Moses raises up other leaders, he will continue to represent the people before God (verse 19). He does not abdicate his role by giving authority to others. Rather, he continues to stand as the chief intermediary between God and the people, and will continue to decide the hardest cases himself. Applying this principle to AI, we can ask what it means to maintain human responsibility. Does it rest ultimately with the user, or with the developer? Does it mean human in the loop always, or just in certain situations? These are challenging questions without straightforward answers. Jethro's advice to Moses helps us see the need to maintain a strong sense of personal responsibility within our sphere of influence, whether than be as a user of AI or as a developer.

Third is education. Before Moses identifies leaders, he must teach the people the statues and instructions of God (verse 20). Often lost in interpreting this passage is its larger context within Exodus. The very next chapter, Exodus 19, initiates God's appearance on Mount Sinai, the giving of the Ten Commandments (Exodus 20), and the set of laws now known as the Covenant Code (Exodus 20:22–23:33). The people and their leaders must receive the law and instruction. For AI this underscores the need for care with AI development, training, and optimization. There must be a strong sense of ethics and the common good, with appropriate regulation. While it is an impossible task to build AI with something like "biblical principles"—which will mean different things to different people—this does mean that people of faith must be involved in ethical AI conversations, informed about relevant policy and its impact, and vocal about what is most important to them and their communities.

Fourth is discernment. Not just anyone is fit to be a leader, but those who are able and morally upright (verse 21). The leaders Moses identifies will demonstrate both knowledge of God's law and good character. Extending to AI means similar discernment when selecting which AI to use. Not all technology is created equal. Some LLMs, for instance, will demonstrate better training or better "character." Christian leaders might investigate which AIs they should prioritize, which to avoid, and which are appropriate only in limited circumstances. Such assessments of the technology should be done with clear values and evaluation criteria. Some things to consider include: the mission of the company that developed it; steps taken to eliminate bias; the environmental impact; how different AIs respond to similar prompts. The key point here is that you can and should evaluate technology.

Jethro's advice to Moses shows us both the need for delegation and the principles undergirding it. These principles include sustainability, responsibility, education, and discernment. This passage shines a light on the circumstances in which this advice might be extended to include AI agents, algorithmic decision-making, and other related technology.

17

Exodus 20:1–17

1 Then God spoke all these words,

2 “I am the LORD your God, who brought you out of the land of Egypt, out of the
house of slavery; 3 you shall have no other gods before me.

4 “You shall not make for yourself an idol, whether in the form of anything that
is in heaven above or that is on the earth beneath or that is in the water under
the earth. 5 You shall not bow down to them or serve them, for I the LORD your
God am a jealous God, punishing children for the iniquity of parents to the third
and the fourth generation of those who reject me 6 but showing steadfast love to
the thousandth generation of those who love me and keep my commandments.

7 “You shall not make wrongful use of the name of the LORD your God, for
the LORD will not acquit anyone who misuses his name.

8 “Remember the Sabbath day and keep it holy. 9 Six days you shall labor and do
all your work. 10 But the seventh day is a Sabbath to the LORD your God; you shall
not do any work—you, your son or your daughter, your male or female slave, your
livestock, or the alien resident in your towns. 11 For in six days the LORD made
heaven and earth, the sea, and all that is in them, but rested the seventh day;
therefore the LORD blessed the Sabbath day and consecrated it.

12 “Honor your father and your mother, so that your days may be long in the land
that the LORD your God is giving you.

13 “You shall not murder.

14 “You shall not commit adultery.

15 “You shall not steal.

16 “You shall not bear false witness against your neighbor.

17 “You shall not covet your neighbor’s house; you shall not covet your neighbor’s
wife, male or female slave, ox, donkey, or anything that belongs to your neighbor.”

17

Exodus 20:1–17
The Ten Commandments and AI

Andrew Witt

For many readers of the Bible, the Ten Commandments (or Ten Words, "Decalogue") provide a basic moral framework for human beings, often equivalent to the natural law. In other words, they are understood as timeless and universal laws for everyone, regardless of time or culture. A quick internet search will show many different links for developing something similar in the AI world, a "Ten Commandments for AI," as it were. But is this the way we should think about the Decalogue? If its purpose in Scripture is *not* a list of rules to live by, then is there another way that the Decalogue can be helpful in developing a basic moral framework for governing our use and development of AI tools?

The Purpose of the Decalogue

To help understand the purpose of the Decalogue we will describe two areas of context that are not often used as part of its framing: ancient legal texts and its surrounding narrative. The first helps us by showing that lists of laws or regulations had a different function in the ancient world than they do now.[1] Most modern people live under a statutory law system, but ancient Near Eastern cultures followed customary law practices.[2] In a statutory system, lists of laws are codified in a text, and that text is understood as the source of law, a complete, self-contained system. In practice, this means that when a governing authority imposes the law on its citizens, it must cite from the codified text. Any loopholes in the law must be filled by new legislation. With customary law, such as what we find in the Pentateuch, lists of laws are not codified in a text; rather, lists of laws or regulations are seen as legal *instruction*, as resources that judges would consult to make informed decisions based on the spirit and customs of their communities. These lists are carefully constructed to give shape to what justice looks like in their society. A just judgment would be seen, then, not in terms of how it follows a binding precedent, but how it aligns with the values or mores of the kingdom. In this different legal context, the Decalogue would have functioned differently than we often assume.

In terms of literary context, the Decalogue itself opens by reminding us of the narrative: the revelation of God's name YHWH and God's deliverance of Israel from Egypt, a house of slavery (Exod 20:1–2). At the outset, then, the Decalogue is presenting us with an alternative life for God's people. In the preceding chapter, as God was inviting them into a new covenantal relationship, he presented Israel with a unique vocational purpose,[3] to be a "kingdom of priests" and a "holy nation" (Exod 19:5–6). Redeemed from Egypt, they were to mediate God's presence and character to the nations, that they too might be blessed (see Gen 12:1–3).[4] The identity of Israel with God was not new, of course, as God had already entered a covenant with the descendants of Abraham (Gen 17), and had already commissioned them with keeping "the way of the Lord by doing righteousness and justice" (Gen 18:19).[5] Their experiences in Egypt, however, would forever shape their life together. Under no circumstances were they to oppress immigrants nor the vulnerable in their midst (see Exod 22:21–24).

Taking this all together, the Decalogue's contextual function was not to give Israel a list of rules to live by but one that would help them understand the character of the Lawgiver (God) and to shape God's moral vision for what Israel's priestly and holy community was to look like.[6] As John Walton notes, the Decalogue describes "the sort of society that Yahweh wishes to establish for the reflection of his identity."[7] By embodying the Decalogue in their life together, the Israelites were reshaping human community in the image of God's redemptive character.[8]

The Decalogue and AI

As we reflect on the Decalogue and AI, then, it would be wrong to simply give a list of ten abstract rules or principles governing the human use and development of AI—however necessary such a list might be for the future of AI.[9] Rather, it is more helpful to give some direction for how AI can be thought about in reference to God's moral vision for his people.

At the outset, it is always important to remember that AI is a human-engineered tool. While running the risk of being too simplistic, generative AI is essentially a highly-advanced pattern recognizer, trained by huge amounts of human data—data that includes all the biases, values, and perspectives that come with human productivity. In other words, its algorithms for decision making have been crafted using the patterns of the world around us rather than God's moral vision for humanity. Does generative AI have the capacity to shape us in a way that images God's redemptive character? At the outset, then, we are met with a very strong caution.

I teach a Ten Commandments course for undergraduate students, and one of the assignments we do in class is to engage a large language model on this very question. I start by asking students to dialogue with a generative AI model, asking it about its purpose. Models typically point to five areas: (1) Assisting human creativity, not replacing but amplifying human imagination; (2) Explaining complex topics or concepts in personalized ways; (3) Simulating scenarios; (4) Automating repetitive or analytical tasks (reports, emails, coding, etc.); and (5) Discovering resources for research. From here, I ask them to further the dialogue by having the model explain different parts of the Decalogue for different audiences, such as a high school level youth group or even a children's Sunday school program. Models usually handle these questions well. Finally, I ask them to have the model "update" the Decalogue for the modern world—what would be Ten Words that give shape to the culture around us. It's fascinating to see its analysis of our culture, almost always replacing one's devotion or obedience to God with a message of inclusive kindness to our neighbors. Any reference to God, in fact, is absent.

The purpose of AI is not, at the outset, in opposition to the purpose of the Decalogue. Rather, much like any other tool, we must be careful to understand its usefulness within the larger moral vision provided by the Decalogue. Generative AI can be quite helpful for productivity and as an analytical tool, but the more we use this tool the better we will understand whether it is helping or hurting us. Is efficiency our highest aim, or is there something important for our minds and hearts about sitting with a topic for a longer period of time? We may come to find that while some tasks can be more efficiently automated, other elements of our human life, especially related to our relationship with God and neighbor, are not about efficiency. When we lose sight of each other as Image Bearers of our Redemptive Creator, our moral vision becomes distorted, opening ourselves up to the very abuses and neglects that the Decalogue is meant to protect us against.

18

1 Kings 3:1–15

1 Solomon made a marriage alliance with Pharaoh king of Egypt; he took Pharaoh's
daughter and brought her into the city of David until he had finished building his
own house and the house of the LORD and the wall around Jerusalem. 2 The people
were sacrificing at the high places, however, because no house had yet been built
for the name of the LORD.

3 Solomon loved the LORD, walking in the statutes of his father David, except that
he sacrificed and offered incense at the high places. 4 The king went to Gibeon
to sacrifice there, for that was the principal high place; Solomon used to offer a
thousand burnt offerings on that altar. 5 At Gibeon the LORD appeared to Solomon
in a dream by night, and God said, "Ask what I should give you." 6 And Solomon
said, "You have shown great and steadfast love to your servant my father David
because he walked before you in faithfulness, in righteousness, and in uprightness
of heart toward you, and you have kept for him this great and steadfast love and
have given him a son to sit on his throne today. 7 And now, O LORD my God, you
have made your servant king in place of my father David, although I am only a
little child; I do not know how to go out or come in. 8 And your servant is in the
midst of the people whom you have chosen, a great people so numerous they
cannot be numbered or counted. 9 Give your servant, therefore, an understanding
mind to govern your people, able to discern between good and evil, for who can
govern this great people of yours?"

10 It pleased the LORD that Solomon had asked this. 11 God said to him, "Because
you have asked this and have not asked for yourself long life or riches or for the
life of your enemies but have asked for yourself understanding to discern what is
right, 12 I now do according to your word. Indeed, I give you a wise and discerning
mind; no one like you has been before you, and no one like you shall arise after
you. 13 I give you also what you have not asked, both riches and honor all your
life; no other king shall compare with you. 14 If you will walk in my ways, keeping
my statutes and my commandments, as your father David walked, then I will
lengthen your life."

[15] Then Solomon awoke; it had been a dream. He came to Jerusalem, where he
stood before the ark of the covenant of the LORD. He offered up burnt offerings
and offerings of well-being and provided a feast for all his servants.

18

1 Kings 3:1–15

The Listening Heart: Discernment in an Age of Intelligent Tools

Ken Penner

When Solomon became king, he faced the kind of challenge that can overwhelm even the gifted: the needs of the people were many, and the responsibility was heavy. In a dream at Gibeon, God invited Solomon to ask for what he wanted. Solomon could have requested the familiar prizes of leadership such as security, victory, long life, or wealth. Instead, he asked for something more searching: an "understanding mind" or, in another translation, a "listening heart" (1 Kings 3:9), so that he could govern well and distinguish between right and wrong.

This is not a request for raw brainpower. It is a request for moral attentiveness: the ability to hear truthfully, judge wisely, and own the weight of responsibility. Solomon is asking to become the kind of leader who can listen past noise, detect what matters, and act in a way that protects life and serves justice.

That posture matters in our own time, as people use automated tools including artificial intelligence (AI). In plain terms, these tools learn patterns from large amounts of information and then produce recommendations or responses based on those patterns. They can be helpful in handling volume: organizing information, speeding up routine work, and offering drafts. The temptation, however, is to confuse speed with wisdom and to treat a confident output as a trustworthy judgment.

But 1 Kings 3 draws a line we cannot afford to blur: intelligence is not the same thing as wisdom. A tool can be impressive and still be morally unformed. It can be quick and still be wrong. It can sound confident and still be careless. God is not impressed by confidence but rather is concerned with goodness: justice, faithfulness, truth, and protection of the vulnerable. Solomon does not ask for more power. He asks for better perception. And he remains accountable for what he does with it.

The story immediately following Solomon's prayer shows what this discernment looks like in public life: two women stand before the king, each claiming to be the mother of the same living child (1 Kings 3:16–28). Solomon does not simply accept the loudest voice.

He does not shrug and say the truth is unknowable. He also does not reduce the case to a cold tally of claims. Instead, he probes in a way that exposes reality, a way that reveals the true thoughts of each woman, and thereby protects and enhances life.

This is an essential ethical lesson for communities that use powerful automated tools: a recommendation is not a verdict, and an output is not a moral judgment. The danger is not that our tools will become too wise, but that we will outsource our own discernment because it is convenient. When a system speaks with confidence, it becomes easy to say, "The system decided." Yet 1 Kings 3 will not allow that escape. Wisdom means staying responsible; it requires listening, testing, judging, and answering for the consequences.

Discernment is therefore essential in a digital world. It is the ability to distinguish truth from falsehood, insight from nonsense, and credible information from misinformation. This skill matters just as much when information comes from automated tools as when it comes from a rumor, a headline, or a powerful person. An unverified claim is dangerous no matter who (or what) delivers it.

Solomon's example invites us to develop a listening heart by asking simple, critical questions. In other words, we imitate Solomon not by seeking faster answers, but by learning how to test claims before we act:

- Check the sources: Where is this coming from? Are sources named? Can they be confirmed?
- Check the evidence: What facts support the claim? Are they sufficient and relevant?
- Check how the idea was developed: What steps connect the information to the conclusion? Does that path make sense?
- Check the reasoning: Do the conclusions actually follow, or are there leaps and contradictions?
- Check assumptions and biases: What is being taken for granted? Whose perspective is centered, and who might be missing or harmed?

These questions are not specific only to technology; they are the training exercises for all kinds of wisdom. Used well, automated tools can become an excellent practice field for discernment because they force us to slow down, verify, and take responsibility for what we pass along. The goal is not to become fearful, but to become faithful: people who listen carefully, test claims, and act justly.

Solomon's prayer is a fitting prayer for our moment. In a world filled with tools that can speak quickly, the people of God are called to cultivate the "listening heart" discernment that loves truth, refuses to surrender responsibility, and seeks justice for real neighbors.

19

Psalm 1:1–6

1 Happy are those
who do not follow the advice of the wicked
or take the path that sinners tread
or sit in the seat of scoffers,
2 but their delight is in the law of the LORD,
and on his law they meditate day and night.
3 They are like trees
planted by streams of water,
which yield their fruit in its season,
and their leaves do not wither.
In all that they do, they prosper.

4 The wicked are not so
but are like chaff that the wind drives away.
5 Therefore the wicked will not stand in the judgment
nor sinners in the congregation of the righteous,
6 for the LORD watches over the way of the righteous,
but the way of the wicked will perish.

19

Psalm 1:1–6
Our Lives and the Lives of Those Around Us

Andrew Witt

The book of Psalms opens with a candid portrait of two ways of life. One way is beneficent, modeled on the way of YHWH, while the other is detrimental, modeled on the way of humanity. The "happy" person will reject the way of humanity but embrace the way of YHWH, delighting in his instruction and ruminating his teaching throughout their days. The first verse portrays this human way using three figures (the wicked, sinners, and scoffers), three activities (walking, standing, and sitting), and three spaces (the counsel, the way, the seat). Each of these figures have a negative connotation in Scripture, usually associated with the harmful and violent treatment of others for the purpose of unjust gain (see Ps 10; Prov 1:9–19, 20–33). The way of YHWH, however, is illustrated by envisioning people as trees that have been transplanted—as people who have been uprooted from one soil and replanted into a different soil. The instruction of YHWH provides an alternative way of life that takes us from one context (the way of humanity) and puts us in another, where our leaves remain green and we bear fruit in season. In other words, our lives are transformed from seeking after our own gain at the expense of others, to providing healing and nourishment for our neighbors (see Ezek 47:12; Rev 22:2). Happiness is not marked merely by inward contentment but by beneficent actions; success is not marked by our bank accounts but by how well our lives impact those around us.

As I have been reflecting on the relationship between Psalm 1 and generative AI, I keep being drawn back to the Hebrew verb *hgh*, which is often translated as "to meditate." Though this translation is very common, it nevertheless obscures that the verbal root is a *speaking* verb—it has as much to do with our mouths as our minds.[1] In Ps 115:7, the psalmist describes idols as objects that cannot *hgh* with their throats. In various passages, the verb *hgh* is used for quiet muttering or murmuring (see Ps 77:13; 143:5), loud proclamation (see Ps 35:28; 37:30; 71:24), and even careful planning (see Ps 38:12 [13]). The futile *hgh*-ing of the peoples in Ps 2:1 provides an important contrast to the constructive *hgh*-ing of the "happy man" in Ps 1. Where their efforts to break out from the sovereign rule of YHWH and his Anointed One are met with the scornful rebuke of YHWH (2:4–6), the *hgh*-ing of the righteous will result in the pouring out of divine blessing through their transplantation along streams of water. And I think what makes this *hgh*-ing so beneficial is that it is not the result of one decision or choice but a lifelong commitment to the way articulated by YHWH in his Torah (Ps 1:2). The kind of rumination that produces the beneficent life is shaped by countless decisions and a life patterned by God's way—it is a proven path that leads to life and not to destruction (Ps 1:6; see Prov 1:17–19).

Generative AI seems to be designed for an efficiency and productivity that circumvents and perhaps even side-steps the kind of careful, slow, day-in, and day-out *hgh*-ing envisioned by Psalm 1. If so, a wholesale embrace of generative AI comes with the dangerous risk of preventing the very means God has put into place to allow for us to experience true happiness via beneficent lives. I'm not convinced that this necessarily has to be the case, but it is a real risk that we must be careful to avoid.

In Paul's letters to Timothy, he reflects on how the last days will be filled with people who love themselves, and while they may have the outward form of godliness, they deny its power (2 Tim 3:1–5). By imagining godliness as "a means of gain," they chase after enrichment of resources and "are trapped by many senseless and harmful desires that plunge people into ruin and destruction" (1 Tim 6:4–10). As we begin to integrate generative AI more into the daily rhythms of life, we must question the long-term effects its new patterns of life are creating within us. Generative AI certainly provides useful tools for productivity and efficiency, but these may teach us to view the world through those lenses only, with an end result that we begin to see the people around us as means to our own profitable ends. Psalm 1 points us in a different direction—a direction that is critical if we would like to find ourselves deeply content and satisfied before God and each other.

20

Proverbs 1:1–7

1 The proverbs of Solomon son of David, king of Israel:

2 For learning about wisdom and instruction,
for understanding words of insight,
3 for gaining instruction in wise dealing,
righteousness, justice, and equity;
4 to teach shrewdness to the simple,
knowledge and prudence to the young—
5 let the wise, too, hear and gain in learning
and the discerning acquire skill,
6 to understand a proverb and a figure,
the words of the wise and their riddles.

7 The fear of the LORD is the beginning of knowledge;
fools despise wisdom and instruction.

20

Proverbs 1:1–7
The Beginning of Wisdom

Nicole L. Tilford

In some respects, the book of Proverbs is one of the closest parallels in the Bible to modern text-based generative AI models. A large amount of information was gathered together from multiple sources, combined, and then used to create something new. In the case of Proverbs, this process occurred sometime between the sixth and fourth centuries BCE. Recognizing the importance of education and traditional knowledge, scribes from Israel and the surrounding regions began gathering together proverbial sayings from their communities. These sayings were largely practical. Work hard and have plenty to eat (e.g., Prov 10:5). Discipline your children (e.g., Prov 13:1). Don't gossip (e.g., Prov 25:8). Such knowledge was gleaned from common experience, from working in the fields, engaging with neighbors, and serving at court. Over time, the scribes wove these disparate sayings into a coherent collection, adding an introduction and reshaping the sayings to reflect their interests. The final book contains, for all practical purposes, the collective knowledge of the entire people of Israel. This aggregated material became a dataset, so to speak, on which the next generation of scribes could be trained.

For the scribes who compiled Proverbs, however, it was not enough to simply collect the knowledge of their people. Memorizing a pithy saying or regurgitating a phrase was not the goal. To have understanding, to be wise, one had to work at it. There was no single answer. Proverbs had to be contextualized. Behavior had to be assessed. The data had to be studied in order to reveal the overall relationship between acts and consequences so that the learned individual could apply the appropriate ethical response to new problems in everyday life. Becoming wise was thus a process, a path the learned individual traversed throughout his or her life. The young had to listen to their elders; elders had to converse with their peers. Both had to make a conscious choice day after day to pay attention and avoid immoral activities. Most importantly, for the scribes who compiled this book, true wisdom was rooted in devotion: "The fear of the Lord is the beginning of knowledge" (Prov 1:7). Being wise meant recognizing God's supreme authority, abiding by his commands, and actively contemplating the natural world he created. Wisdom was not a quick answer. It was a way of life.

Current text-based generative AI technology is transactional. Ask a question. Receive an answer. Behind the scenes, sophisticated computer codes analyze preexisting data to extract underlying patterns, formulate predictions, and generate seemingly novel responses. But the average user is not privy to any of that. The technology provides a shortcut that, on the surface, appears quick and efficient but is actually quite dangerous. Without introspection, without contemplation, the ability to think for oneself, to understand complex ideas, and to apply that understanding to new situations erodes. The savvy user might ask a more sophisticated question and be able to tell accurate responses from hallucinations. But the result is basically the same. Information without understanding.

The scribes of Proverbs could not have imagined the technology at our fingertips. Yet their approach to wisdom might provide a helpful way for modern people to engage with these innovations. Like the proverbs gathered from the ancient people of Israel, the texts that have been used to train generative AI programs reflect the collective knowledge of society, but the answers generated, however helpful, are only starting points. The wise individual should consider whether the received information is accurate and appropriately fits the context. He or she should ask further questions, seek additional perspectives, and continually reflect upon the complexities of the world. True understanding does not come from quick answers. It requires effort and takes a lifetime to learn.

21

Proverbs 4:1–9

1 Listen, children, to a father's instruction,
and be attentive, that you may gain insight,
2 for I give you good precepts:
do not forsake my teaching.
3 When I was a son with my father,
tender and my mother's favorite,
4 he taught me and said to me,
"Let your heart hold fast my words;
keep my commandments and live.
5 Get wisdom; get insight: do not forget nor turn away
from the words of my mouth.
6 Do not forsake her, and she will keep you;
love her, and she will guard you.
7 The beginning of wisdom is this: get wisdom,
and whatever else you get, get insight.
8 Prize her highly, and she will exalt you;
she will honor you if you embrace her.
9 She will place on your head a fair garland;
she will bestow on you a beautiful crown."

21

Proverbs 4:1–9
An Ongoing Test of Wisdom

S. Joshua Swamidass

Scripture does not assume that understanding comes naturally. It must be pursued. It must be learned. Without it, even sincere judgments go astray. Proverbs warns against answering before listening (18:13) and against accepting the first explanation without testing it (18:17). Wisdom requires more than good intentions. It requires attention, patient learning, and the discipline of making the right distinctions.

This is especially relevant in how we speak about artificial intelligence (AI). Many voices speak with confidence about AI—what it is, what it will become, and what we should do about it—while still misunderstanding it. If Proverbs is right, this is not merely an intellectual mistake. It is a failure of wisdom. The rise of AI is a test of our wisdom.

Understanding and Wisdom

In Proverbs, understanding is not abstract knowledge. It is the disciplined practice of seeing clearly and acting well. It means listening before answering, testing claims before accepting them, and recognizing when differences matter.

Scripture itself resists simple, universal rules: "Answer not a fool according to his folly . . . Answer a fool according to his folly" (Prov 26:4–5). These are not mere contradictions to be resolved by a single rule. Whether you answer or not, there are risks—you may become like the fool, or you may leave him wise in his own eyes. Wisdom lies in discerning which risk matters in the moment. As Scripture elsewhere reminds us, there is "a time for every matter under heaven" (Eccl 3:1).

This kind of wisdom depends on careful distinctions. The wise person does not overgeneralize or rush to judgment. Instead, he or she learns to recognize kinds, contexts, and consequences. This posture stands in tension with how AI is often discussed. We speak quickly, generalize broadly, and draw firm conclusions about things we do not yet understand. Consider a few examples.

What We Call "AI"

"Artificial intelligence" is not one thing. It is a label we place over a wide range of very different tools. At its core, much of what we call AI is a kind of numerical dance—systems detecting patterns in data and acting on them at scale. Despite this shared core, "AI" may refer to spam filters that filter out unwanted email, recommendation systems that suggest what to watch or buy, image-recognition systems that help identify tumors in medical scans, large language models that generate text, or autonomous vehicles that navigate roads, among many others.

These systems do not merely differ in degree. They differ in kind. At one level, they may rely on similar computational techniques. But in ways that matter, each operates differently, serves a distinct purpose, and raises its own set of questions. A system that recommends a movie is not the same as one that assists a physician. A tool that generates text is not the same as one that controls a vehicle.

Some forms of AI raise questions about whether the image of God is unique to humans—or even what we mean by the image of God. Others raise more focused questions about ethics and policy. Still others press on learning and work, touching assumptions about how we understand our future.

Yet we often speak about all of these under a single label, as if they were the same thing. This lack of distinction produces confusion. Concerns that apply to one type of system are transferred to another. Hopes for one application are assumed for all. Without careful categorization, our judgments about AI will be imprecise at best and misleading at worst.

A Moving Target

Even if we understood AI well today, that understanding would quickly become outdated. The field is changing rapidly. New systems are being developed, existing systems are gaining capabilities, and new uses are emerging. We are not evaluating a stable, singular object, but a moving field. The questions we ask today may not be the ones we need to ask tomorrow. The risks and opportunities shift as the technology develops.

At present, there is good reason to think that no current AI is conscious or sentient in a way that would give rise to moral responsibilities toward the system itself. But AI is not static. It is evolving in capability and appearing in new forms. It is possible that this assessment could change—that a type of AI could emerge to which we might owe some form of ethical consideration.

Proverbs describes wisdom as a continuing process: "Let the wise hear and increase in learning" (1:5). Wisdom is not achieved once and for all. It grows through ongoing attention and correction. When we treat AI as static, we make judgments that quickly become outdated or irrelevant.

Context Matters

The same system can be used in ways that are beneficial, harmful, or somewhere in between. One AI system might assist a physician in diagnosis, while another might be used to spread misinformation. It might support learning, or it might be used to bypass it.

We often want simple rules: embrace AI or reject it, trust it or fear it. But Scripture cautions against this kind of simplicity. Proverbs 26:4–5 gives two opposite instructions side by side: do not answer a fool according to his folly, and answer a fool according to his folly. The point is not contradiction, but discernment. Whether you answer or not, there are risks. The same situation can require different responses depending on the circumstances.

Wisdom, then, is not the application of simple rules, but the practice of fitting judgment to the situation. Evaluating AI therefore requires attention to specifics—what the system is, how it works, and how it is used. Broad generalizations are rarely sufficient.

What We Do Not Know

Some of the most important questions about AI remain unanswered. Can a machine possess something like a mind? Could an artificial system bear the image of God? These are profound questions that invite serious reflection.

At present, we do not know. We can speculate and explore, but we should be cautious about declaring certainty where understanding is still developing. Some speak confidently about what AI can never become. Others are equally confident about what it inevitably will become. Both claims outrun our understanding.

Here, humility is not weakness. It is a recognition of reality. When knowledge is limited and the subject is complex, wisdom entails this restraint.

Saying "We Do Not Yet Know"

In a culture that rewards quick answers, "We don't know" can feel like failure. But, in fact, recognizing what we don't know is intrinsic to the task of seeking understanding. In this way, this satisfying answer can be the beginning of wisdom, the humble starting point from where we might seek—and maybe even find—understanding.

This humble posture does not mean disengagement. We can and should seek out answers by asking better questions, seeking deeper understanding, and remaining open to correction. But this all takes time, and premature certainty is a misleading trap.

This posture of seeking understanding is what it means to be wise. Before we evaluate artificial intelligence—before we declare what it is, what it means, or what should be done—we are called first to understand.

Conclusion

AI is often presented as a defining issue of our time. It raises important questions about technology, society, and what it means to be human. These questions deserve careful attention. But before we rush to answer them, Scripture directs us to a prior and ongoing task: "Get understanding." This direction is acutely important as we engage with AI, because AI is not a single, simple, static thing. It is a diverse and rapidly changing set of tools used in many ways. Without understanding this complexity, our judgments will be shallow and our conclusions unreliable.

In this way, AI is a fundamental test of our wisdom. Will we seek understanding first, or speak before we have understood? Will we make careful distinctions, or settle for easy generalizations? Will we adjust our conclusions as the subject itself changes?

Before we decide what AI means for the future, we should first—and continually—seek to understand what it is. Scripture gives that priority a name: wisdom.

22

Ecclesiastes 1:3–11

3 What do people gain from all the toil
  at which they toil under the sun?
4 A generation goes, and a generation comes,
  but the earth remains forever.
5 The sun rises, and the sun goes down
  and hurries to the place where it rises.
6 The wind blows to the south
  and goes around to the north;
round and round goes the wind,
  and on its circuits the wind returns.
7 All streams run to the sea,
  but the sea is not full;
to the place where the streams flow,
  there they continue to flow.
8 All things are wearisome,
  more than one can express;
the eye is not satisfied with seeing
  or the ear filled with hearing.
9 What has been is what will be,
  and what has been done is what will be done;
  there is nothing new under the sun.
10 Is there a thing of which it is said,
  "See, this is new"?
It has already been
  in the ages before us.
11 The people of long ago are not remembered,
  nor will there be any remembrance
of people yet to come
  by those who come after them.

22

Ecclesiastes 1:3–11

There Is Nothing New under the Sun

Nicole L. Tilford

Ecclesiastes is a pessimistic book. In it, a narrator known as the Teacher considers the nature of human life and concludes that most human activities are pointless. Whether one is wise or foolish, rich or poor, weak or strong, everyone dies in the end (Eccl 2:14–15). The wicked are rewarded, and the righteous fall to despair (Eccl 8:14). Accomplishments are forgotten, and wealth is left for the next generation to enjoy (Eccl 6:1–6).

The prologue to the book reflects this pessimism. Opening the book with a poetic flourish, the prologue describes the natural operations of the world. The sun rises and sets, but it does not reach a destination. Rivers flow to the ocean, but they do not run dry, and the sea does not fill. Humans work all day, but nothing new is achieved. "What has been is what will be, and what has been done is what will be done; there is nothing new under the sun" (Eccl 1:9).

Contemporary generative AI seems to embody this situation. A large amount of data is used to train these programs, but the technology does not actually generate anything "new." It gives the appearance of novelty without exhibiting any true originality. The ideas are derivative. The information, if accurate, can already be found in preexisting sources. The words are a conglomeration of previous diction. Text is recycled, often without attribution, such that those who produced the material in the first place are forgotten. The people that made this innovation possible are devalued. As the technology becomes more pervasive in daily life, the situation compounds. Human labor is replaced by digital product. Nothing authentic is created, and the human element is lost.

The prologue to Ecclesiastes does not provide an answer to this pessimistic state. The Teacher throws up his hands and surrenders to the idea that all human toil is futile. It would be tempting to follow the Teacher into his depression. Perhaps one day technology *will* replace human labor. Our toils will be forgotten, and all that we currently occupy ourselves with will be inherited by our technological offspring. Elsewhere in Ecclesiastes, however, the Teacher seems to imply that there may be a solution to this problem or at least a temporary reprieve from it. "There is nothing better for mortals," says the Teacher, "than to eat and drink and find enjoyment in their toil" (Eccl 2:24; see also 3:12–13; 5:18–19; etc.). If technology is able to relieve us from tedious tasks, we may find time for more fulfilling pursuits. Instead of being bogged down in spreadsheets or data sets, we could relax outdoors or with friends. We could concentrate on fixing the ills of society and bringing relief to the suffering of others. We could focus our attention on a higher purpose.

"What do people gain from all the toil at which they toil under the sun?" (Eccl 1:3). That depends. Do we follow the Teacher into despair or shift our perspective? Do we give up or seek more worthwhile endeavors? There may be nothing new under the sun, and our toils may be a chasing after the wind. But it need not all be in vain.

23

Luke 2:41–52

[41] Now every year his parents went to Jerusalem for the festival of the Pass-
over. [42] And when he was twelve years old, they went up as usual for the festi-
val. [43] When the festival was ended and they started to return, the boy Jesus stayed
behind in Jerusalem, but his parents were unaware of this. [44] Assuming that he
was in the group of travelers, they went a day's journey. Then they started to
look for him among their relatives and friends. [45] When they did not find him,
they returned to Jerusalem to search for him. [46] After three days they found him
in the temple, sitting among the teachers, listening to them and asking them
questions. [47] And all who heard him were amazed at his understanding and his
answers. [48] When his parents saw him they were astonished, and his mother said
to him, "Child, why have you treated us like this? Your father and I have been anx-
iously looking for you." [49] He said to them, "Why were you searching for me? Did
you not know that I must be in my Father's house?" [50] But they did not understand
what he said to them. [51] Then he went down with them and came to Nazareth
and was obedient to them, and his mother treasured all these things in her heart.
[52] And Jesus increased in wisdom and in years and in divine and human favor.

23

Luke 2:41–52
Normal Human Growth

John Dyer

Science fiction books and movies often imagine a future where humans receive enhancements or download skills, instantly giving them new mental and physical abilities. But if such technology actually existed, would it be good for us?

If there was ever a human that had access to such immediate augmentation, it would have been Jesus. Christians believe that Jesus is the eternal Son of God, with the same fully divine nature as the Father and Spirit before time began. Then, in the incarnation, he took on a fully human nature, one that is exactly like us in every way, except he did not sin.

Luke's Gospel uniquely emphasizes just how human Jesus really was. One way he does that is through several scenes in the opening chapters that depict Jesus going through the normal human processes of growing physically and intellectually, both of which take time. In Luke 1, we see Jesus growing physically in Mary's womb (Luke 1:41). Later when he was presented at the temple, we see this physical development continue as "the child grew and became strong" (Luke 2:40). Then as a twelve-year-old, he returned to the temple, this time "sitting among the teachers, listening to them and asking them questions" (Luke 2:46). At the end of that scene, we learn that "Jesus grew in wisdom and stature" (Luke 2:52).

In these brief glimpses of Jesus's childhood, we see that Jesus experienced a period of normal human growth. Luke also implies that it is quite normal for wisdom to develop over time—even the boy Jesus asks questions in order to learn (Luke 2:46). Jesus, although the God-man, chose to discover his creation as a human would, rather than choosing to know everything immediately. Jesus could have merely leaned into his divine nature to know everything—something he does on occasion as an adult (John 2:24–25)—but when he took on "the very nature of a servant . . . human likeness" (Phil 2:7), he chose to fully submit to the general parameters of human limitation and finitude. This meant that he took time to ask questions, listen, and grow, in a sinless way, such that people marveled at his accelerated growth (Luke 2:47). For Jesus to be authentically human and understand our life, he chose to acquire knowledge and wisdom in the slow, sometimes awkward way humans do.

However, in this era, while we are rightly interested in "machine learning," we are not always as interested in human learning—by which I mean the slow, enriching development of wisdom that Luke depicts in his Gospel. As a society, we spend enormous time and resources training models to grow ever larger, smarter, and more capable, but we are less willing to expend personal effort on our own intellectual and spiritual growth.

AI tools offer us tremendous power, and we can and should harness that power to do good things that honor God and love our neighbor. Such tools can enhance Bible translation, aid in medical diagnoses, and automate repetitive and laborious tasks, opening up new avenues for caring for those around us. And yet, as we take advantage of these enhancements to our abilities and access to knowledge, we must not neglect our own human design that develops over time and with others.

We understand this intuitively when it comes to our physical abilities. We know that when a machine carries us 26.2 miles, we have not gained the ability to do that ourselves. Instead, if we want to become a person who can actually run that far, we must practice the regular discipline of running, building physical strength and endurance over many long months. As machines allow us to go beyond our physical abilities, AI systems often allow us to go beyond our mental abilities. They can respond to nearly any question we ask, solve an increasing number of problems we offer, and create most visuals we describe. But when the output is ready, we will not have grown or gained new mental capacities. In fact, an increasing number of studies indicate that our mental capacities can atrophy over time when we become dependent on AI systems.

This doesn't mean we should never use machines for intellectual work, any more than we should never use bikes, cars, or airplanes for travel. But as we seek to develop and expand our own internal capacities, we should select some areas of our lives where we choose not to use a tool to get immediate results. In the physical world, this might be taking walks or a favorite exercise. In an age of intelligent machines, this might look like brainstorming with pen and paper first, engaging with people around us, or trying to solve a problem own our own. Machines are good gift from God, but if we want to be like Jesus, we must sometimes make the choice to engage in the slow human process of asking questions, listening, and growing.

24

Philippians 3:10–16

10 I want to know Christ and the power of his resurrection and the sharing of
his sufferings by becoming like him in his death, 11 if somehow I may attain the
resurrection from the dead.

12 Not that I have already obtained this or have already reached the goal, but
I press on to lay hold of that for which Christ has laid hold of me. 13 Brothers
and sisters, I do not consider that I have laid hold of it, but one thing I have laid
hold of: forgetting what lies behind and straining forward to what lies ahead, 14 I
press on toward the goal, toward the prize of the heavenly call of God in Christ
Jesus. 15 Let those of us, then, who are mature think this way, and if you think
differently about anything, this, too, God will reveal to you. 16 Only let us hold
fast to what we have attained.

24

Philippians 3:10–16

Best, Not Better

Ed Gerber

AI can do many things better than humans—with greater efficiency, polish, accuracy. The list of executable tasks is extensive and growing. AI is a marvel. Even now, AI controlled robotic devices do industrial and medical tasks better than human beings. In time, these machines will likely do domestic and other tasks better too. But does the fact that AI can do tasks better than humans constitute an argument that we should defer our tasks to AI? To let it write our papers? Our poems? To eventually let it tend our gardens?

That depends.

Reflecting on his own identity as one who by suffering with Christ may "somehow attain to the resurrection from the dead," the Apostle Paul insists: "Not that I have already obtained all this, or have already arrived at my goal, but I press on to take hold of that for which Christ took hold of me" (Phil 3:10–14).

Christ took hold of those who trust in him not only that we may be clothed with a new resurrected materiality when he returns; he took hold of us so that, as those already united to the resurrected Christ,[1] we may live a resurrection life today, the life of the Spirit (Rom 6:4).

The question, therefore, is not "Can AI do this better and should we, therefore, best let AI do it?" The question is, "Is allowing AI to do this 'better' in *our* best interest? Or is it jeopardizing distinctively human goods, not least of all our development into all that Christ has taken hold of us to be?"

For example, Genesis portrays human work before the Fall as an intrinsic good—indeed, an act of worship.[2] The degree to which we allow AI to do our work for us, then, is a question of what is wise for our own wellbeing, not whether AI can do it better than us. To allow AI to transform us wholesale into *homo otiose* (humans of leisure) would not be for our *best*. This does not imply, of course, that we fail to distinguish between the ennobling 'work' of humans prior to the Fall and the enervating 'toil' of the post-fall world (cf. Gen 2:15; 3:19a). Substituting AI and technological innovation for the latter, for example, as made possible with modern farming equipment, may contribute rather than detract from human flourishing.

Or take another example. Bodily connection between humans is good, vital to human flourishing. David Brooks elucidates the irreducible value of eye-contact, skin-to-skin contact, smell, and vocal attunement in facilitating secure attachment between mother and child.[3] A sophisticated AI servomechanism that could get infants to nurse better without the nursing mother would thus not be in best interest of that child.

Wisdom is key. To choose to use AI is not a choice between black and white, good and evil, right and wrong. It is a choice between comparatives and superlatives, betters and bests. The prudence of the author of Ecclesiastes must become ours: there is a time for everything, including a time to use AI and a time not to use it (c.f., Ecclesiastes 3). Wisdom must discern what time it is. When the expedience and technical superiority of using AI subverts our own becoming what we are in Christ, we must choose to jettison the better for the best.

25

1 Thessalonians 5:19–22

[19] Do not quench the Spirit. [20] Do not despise prophecies, [21] but test everything;
hold fast to what is good; [22] abstain from every form of evil.

25

1 Thessalonians 5:19–22
Test Everything

Jay Kranda

In 2025, ChatGPT alone responded to around 2.5 billion prompts every day.[1] This rapid adoption of AI is more than a trend; it is a cultural shift. As followers of Christ, we are called to provide clarity on how to thrive in the midst of this integration, while ensuring our faith does not retreat into the shadows but stands firmly in the light. We live in the "middle phase" of God's Kingdom—a season where sin has "already" been paid for, but its effects are "not yet" fully removed.[2] In this broken world, our calling is to shed light where truth is lacking. There *are* answers to the tough questions of an ever-changing AI-integrated world. Recognizing that all truth comes from the Creator and as a result there is a "right way to live" on this side of eternity, simply avoiding these questions will not work.

First Thessalonians offers a blueprint for engaging a rapidly changing culture. Ancient Thessalonica was a cosmopolitan hub. It was a collision of Greek cults, diverse philosophies, Egyptian mysticism, and a burgeoning Jewish community.[3] The young church there faced intense pressure, wrestling with pagan immorality and confusion over spiritual gifts. Into this noise, the Apostle Paul provided a specific mandate in 1 Thessalonians 5:19–22: "Do not quench the Spirit. Do not despise prophecies, but test everything; hold fast to what is good; abstain from every form of evil."

While we often read this as a general call to be careful, scholars like Eugene Boring note that this maxim applied specifically to the "inspired revelations" emerging in the church's worship. Paul was responding to "counterfeit prophets" who were delivering oracular-type messages to the community. His instruction was to hit pause on every prophetic word until the community had a chance to evaluate it using the Holy Spirit and truth God had already spoken.

Today, AI performs a remarkably similar "oracular" function. We turn to Large Language Models (LLMs) for answers to life's deep questions, seeking guidance that often feels authoritative, yet lacks a foundation in truth. To "test everything" in an AI-integrated world, we must apply Paul's rigor to three specific areas:

The Fallibility of the Utterance (*Mistruth*): AI can be wrong. LLMs confabulate and misreport facts, as their reasoning is based on information the model indexed online in conjunction with the humans that ranked the content for the model to learn.[4] Consider how an AI "learns" humor. A model may analyze a hundred jokes, which are then ranked by humans from most to least funny. By repeating this process, the model identifies patterns in human preference and eventually replicates them without further human input. Consequently, we must critically evaluate AI outputs, recognizing that these models generate responses based on mathematical probability rather than a grounded grasp of the truth. Just as the Thessalonians had to discern between true prophecy and counterfeit oracles, we must hold every word an AI utters in check and remember how the model "learned" the outputted response.

The Danger of "Oracular" Dependence (*Distraction*): Like any pursuit, these models can become "idols" that obstruct our relationship with God. While the human capacity for rapid learning is a gift, AI has introduced a shadow side: "doom learning." Much like "doom scrolling," this involves spiraling into an infinite loop of information where the rush of the "deep dive" leads to the neglect of actual responsibilities.[5] In this scenario, we prioritize infinite prompt engagement over working out our other responsibilities God entrusts to us.[6] We must remain vigilant and recognize when AI begins to function as a false guide that cause spiritual atrophy through addiction and obstructs our relationship with the Creator.

The Absence of Spirit-Led Discernment (Disconnections): While it may sound like the plot of a science fiction novel, an increasing number of people are substituting human connection for AI companionship. An example is the recent rise in people using AI for therapy.[7] At present, an AI therapist offers a judgment-free environment, and therefore lacks the ability and wisdom to provide biblical correction. An AI therapist can reaffirm more of what one wants to hear and not provide specific customized guidelines that can lead to a better life. Biblical community is not solely encouraging, but also challenge us to live to God's biblical standard. A brother or sister in Christ can discern when technology is hindering our walk or when a model's inherent bias is leading us astray. Paul challenged the Thessalonians as a friend who loved them enough to point out their errors. Platforms like Nomi, Replika, and Character.ai are increasingly filling a void that God designed to be filled with the body of Christ.

The influence of AI will likely expand exponentially in the coming decades. Our task is not to retreat into the shadows, but to ensure our faith stands firmly in the light. By treating AI outputs as "prophetic" claims that require rigorous testing rather than immediate acceptance, we follow the pragmatic approach Paul laid out for the Thessalonians. We must be willing to hit pause, using the wisdom of the Bible and dwelling in biblical community to discern what is true, holding fast only to that which is good.

26

Hebrews 4:12–13

[12] Indeed, the word of God is living and active and sharper than any two-edged
sword, piercing until it divides soul from spirit, joints from marrow; it is able to
judge the thoughts and intentions of the heart. [13] And before him no creature is
hidden, but all are naked and laid bare to the eyes of the one to whom we must
render an account.

26

Hebrews 4:12–13
The Digital Wilderness

Jay Kranda

The Epistle to the Hebrews remains one of the most enigmatic texts of the New Testament. Its author is unknown, its original audience remains nameless, and their specific location is lost to history. Among the author's more mysterious arguments is the invocation of Melchizedek—an obscure priest-king from Genesis (Gen 14; Ps 110). The author of Hebrews uses this figure to establish Jesus as a "great high priest" (Heb. 4:14).

Hebrews 4:12–13 occurs in the first part of the text, just after the author's warning that Israel did not enter the Promised Land immediately because of their lack of faithfulness and obedience to God (Heb 3). The author emphasizes the importance of resting on the Sabbath as one of the commandments and notes that the ancient Israelites struggled to obey this command. A heart that is hardened does not listen to God, but a heart that is fully aligned to God submits to a new way of living. The Israelites failed to enter the Promised Land because they lost sight of God's voice amidst the trials of the desert.

Today, we find ourselves in a digital wilderness. A new cultural assumption has taken root: the belief that artificial intelligence will eventually supersede humanity. Top engineers, like Anthony Levandowski from Google, are making headlines by calling AI a god.[1] To grant AI the status of a "god" is not merely a technological prediction; it is a theological claim that denies the unique sovereignty of the Creator. Such a move reveals a "calloused heart" similar to that of the ancient Israelites—a heart that prefers a visible, manufactured power over the invisible, eternal God. While AI can store and synthesize an infinite sea of data, it remains a shadow of human creation, not a spark of the divine. Something that can be deactivated with a switch is no deity. Just as the readers of Hebrews forgot the truths of the Old Testament about what God had done and was doing, we, as followers of Jesus in the AI moment, keep foregrounded in our minds and hearts the limitations of this created technology. If we lose this perspective, we risk repeating the sins of the wilderness: settling for a lesser version of truth and missing the "rest" found only in the Creator.

When contemplating this synthetic future through the lens of Hebrews, two primary convictions emerge.

First, truth is anchored in the character of God (cf. John 17:17), and thus we use the Bible as a filter to guide our response to new technology. The readers of Hebrews relied on the old stories from the Torah, the history books, and the Prophets, as well as the newly circulating writings of disciples in the 1st century. Today, these Scriptures are unified and instantly accessible, the Old Testament and New Testament, conveniently together, as an app on our phone. AI speaks a form of truth, one that is incomplete as it is ultimately an amalgamation of human knowledge. We must use the Bible as the ultimate filter, recognizing that while an AI model can summarize information, it cannot mediate divine truth.

Second, we must recognize AI as a potential idol. While God sees all and knows all, AI is merely another creation of humanity, fashioned by the limited intellect of God's created beings. To stand in "awe" of a prompt's response is to risk a modern form of idolatry. Humanity loves to worship things they think are greater than themselves, but AI is not greater than humanity. Recognizing these dangers does not negate AI's potential as a remarkable feat of ingenuity. Rather, it is a reminder that our wonder must be disciplined. We must put aside the "awe" of the machine to maintain the "fear" of the Lord, actively discerning falsehoods and refusing to let a tool dictate our moral path.

Ultimately, the book of Hebrews argues that Jesus alone is worthy of adoration. He is not a "created technology" or a refined trained model; he is the Word in human form (Heb. 2:14), the eternal priest (Heb. 7:16), and the perfect sacrifice. The technological "inflection point" we currently inhabit is not a surprise to God. He understands the human tendency to chase progress at the expense of his promises. We can avoid the sins of our ancestors by allowing the Word of God to guide us in how we embrace AI in our daily lives. By looking to the "cloud of witnesses" in Hebrews 11, figures like Noah, Abraham, and Sarah who remained faithful in their own moments of uncertainty, we can navigate the age of AI with a faith that is grounded in the eternal, rather than the artificial.

27

1 John 4:1–6

1 Beloved, do not believe every spirit, but test the spirits to see whether they are
from God, for many false prophets have gone out into the world. 2 By this you
know the Spirit of God: every spirit that confesses that Jesus Christ has come in
the flesh is from God, 3 and every spirit that does not confess Jesus is not from God.
And this is the spirit of the antichrist, of which you have heard that it is coming,
and now it is already in the world. 4 Little children, you are from God and have
conquered them, for the one who is in you is greater than the one who is in the
world. 5 They are from the world; therefore what they say is from the world, and
the world listens to them. 6 We are from God. Whoever knows God listens to us,
and whoever is not from God does not listen to us. From this we know the spirit
of truth and the spirit of error.

27

1 John 4:1–6
Testing the Spirits

James F. McGrath

There is perhaps no more pressing concern in the era of AI than whom and what to trust. When discussing the letters of Paul and other parts of the New Testament, scholars highlight that the word translated as "faith" in many English Bibles is focused on *trust* rather than assent to doctrinal positions or merely holding beliefs. Yet in 1 John 4:1, relatively few English translations render its warning in terms of not *trusting* every spirit.

As 1 John 4 progresses, the focus shifts onto false prophets, the human vessels through which deceitful spirits that are not of God give utterance. The author of the letter is aware that, while human beings can be deceptive in and of themselves, those with a special authority, and those who are perceived to be inspired, are especially dangerous if they use that status to promote falsehood. A key point is that no supernatural being is worthy of being trusted simply by virtue of that status, any more than a human authority is. We have not only the right but the duty to question and evaluate even claims with a supernatural source.

Artificial intelligence (AI) is not a good label for the technology that we have, but whatever one calls it, it is often viewed as though it were, if not a supernatural authority, then certainly a super-human one. The teaching in 1 John 4 certainly seems applicable.

One can ask an AI chatbot whether Jesus Christ has come in the flesh. If it happens to give the right answer when you do so, that is not sufficient grounds for issuing a blanket declaration that this technology is from God and thenceforth to be trustworthy in all its outputs. I doubt that the author of 1 John meant that any prophet who affirms Jesus Christ has come in the flesh is guaranteed to be truthful in all other matters. That was just the pressing issue in the author's time.

The point is that Christians must test the spirits, and the way to do that was not to immediately believe the outputs of prophets, but to ask follow-up questions. It is guaranteed that if you do that sufficiently with AI chatbots, not taking them at their word but checking whether the text they generate corresponds to reality, their current propensity for fabrication will be revealed. They regularly utter falsehood with the confidence of a prophet. It is crucially important that they not be given the authority of one. But if you cannot shake the sense that they have prophetic insight, or are dealing with others who assume that to be the case, at least you can raise the possibility that they might be "false prophets," which doesn't mean that they always deceive, but that they sometimes do.

In the case of generative AI, the reason why they utter falsehood is not because they are possessed by a spirit that is not from God. The reason is that there is no consciousness there, whether human, angelic, or demonic. They produce text through algorithmic processes. We have not discovered an algorithm that will perfectly guarantee factuality and accuracy.

If supernatural minds need to be tested and questioned, and may be judged untrustworthy and deceptive as a result, how much more so a mechanical process stringing words together based on language patterns in its training data? Chatbots are not our first creations to which we have been able to pose questions and receive answers. We can ask a Magic 8 Ball questions about Christology, and it may not get them wrong. Chatbots, to be sure, are a far more sophisticated and impressive technology. Yet in both cases, unless we take the time to understand the technology in question, we may trust it in ways that it does not deserve and that it is not safe to do so.

The ramifications of what the author of 1 John says are astonishing and important. Even supernatural revelation cannot be presumed trustworthy. The Scriptures contain stories not only of deceptive spirits, but of a spirit being sent by God to deliberately mislead (1 Kgs 22:22). As a result, there needs to be another means of determining what is true. If spirits need to be held to that standard, so too do chatbots. This principle has nothing to do with our ability to comprehend the nature of non-human minds, whether angelic or artificial. Whether angels or machines have free will or merely follow their programming, and whether we can confidently answer such questions, the need for discernment remains just the same.

In the era of generative AI, the skill to discern between truth and error has not become obsolete. On the contrary, it is more crucially important and essential now than ever before.

Here is perhaps the most crucial thing to understand: Whatever the standard by which you judge doctrinal or moral correctness, an AI chatbot will likely sometimes match it and at other times will not. Even if you never spot any output that is at odds with your understanding of sound doctrine, it is important to understand that the reason for this has nothing to do with the ability of AI to discern religious (or any other sort of) truth. It has no mechanism for doing that. Its outputs reflect the relationship between words in its training data in relation to the words of your input. Its output is based on rules as well as probabilities. Because of this, the fact that it gave you an answer yesterday that you determined to be correct is no guarantee that it will do the same today or tomorrow.

Ultimately, AI chatbots are a very different sort of problem from deceitful spirits and false prophets. They do not actively seek to mislead, because they do not actively seek to do anything. Yet in another sense, the problem is the same. Neither false prophets, nor well-intentioned but poorly-informed preachers turning to speech-imitating software in crafting their sermons, are harmful to your spiritual life unless you accept them as authorities and trust their utterances without question. Thus, the solution to navigating the spiritual challenge of the era of generative AI is still that advocated in the First Letter of John: Do not trust. *Test.*

Part 4

AI and Ethics

28

Exodus 21:28–36

[28] "When an ox gores a man or a woman to death, the ox shall be stoned, and its
flesh shall not be eaten, but the owner of the ox shall not be liable. [29] If the ox has
been accustomed to gore in the past and its owner has been warned but did not
restrain it, and it kills a man or a woman, the ox shall be stoned, and its owner
also shall be put to death. [30] If a ransom is imposed on the owner, then the owner
shall pay whatever is imposed for the redemption of the victim's life. [31] If it gores a
boy or a girl, the owner shall be dealt with according to this same rule. [32] If the ox
gores a male or female slave, the owner shall pay to the slaveowner thirty shekels
of silver, and the ox shall be stoned.

[33] "If someone leaves a pit open or digs a pit and does not cover it, and an ox or a
donkey falls into it, [34] the owner of the pit shall make restitution, giving money to
its owner but keeping the dead animal.

[35] "If someone's ox hurts the ox of another, so that it dies, then they shall sell the
live ox and divide the price of it, and the dead animal they shall also divide. [36] But
if it was known that the ox was accustomed to gore in the past and its owner did
not restrain it, the owner shall restore ox for ox but keep the dead animal.

28

Exodus 21:28–36
Responsibility in an Age of AI

Marcus Schwarting

In Exodus 21:28–36, we are introduced to important case law. If an ox gores a man or woman to death, the animal is to be stoned, and its flesh not eaten. Yet the owner is acquitted unless the ox had a known history of violence and the owner failed to restrain it. In that case, the owner bears liability and may face severe penalties. The principle is plain: responsibility is not exhausted at the point of creation or ownership. It extends into knowledge, negligence, and response.

Old Testament scholars note that these laws are not merely primitive regulations but moral calibrations of responsibility within a covenantal community. As Christopher J.H. Wright observes, Israel's case laws "protect the vulnerable by locating responsibility where power and knowledge reside."[1] Similarly, John H. Walton emphasizes that such laws embed a theology of ordered responsibility: human agents are accountable for foreseeable harm arising from what they control.[2]

For AI developers, this passage delivers an unsettling clarity. For them, these "oxen" are large, powerful, and increasingly autonomous AI models. When deployed into production, their effects can be visible at scale. Like an ox, they may harm. The question of Exodus is not whether harm can occur, but reparations once the harm has occurred, and the responsibility of those who knew about the danger beforehand.

Exodus 21:28 suggests an initial threshold: harm is a serious moral event. The ox is destroyed and the community acknowledges the gravity of the loss. The underlying moral principle of this passage implies that developers cannot treat a propensity for harm as an acceptable externality. A fatality involving a self-driving system, such as those reported in connection with systems developed by companies like Tesla[3], is not just a statistical anomaly. It is a moral rupture that demands attention, transparency, and immediate mitigation.

Some technical literature on AI safety echoes this.[4] Real-world deployment introduces distributional shifts and unforeseen failure modes, so the moment a system causes harm, the responsible reaction is not to defend aggregate performance metrics but to reassess the system's readiness for deployment.

The law sharpens in Exodus 21:29: if the ox was known to gore and the owner failed to restrain it, liability transfers decisively to the owner. In AI development terms, once a failure mode is identified (via internal testing, user reports, or public incidents), developers are no longer in the realm of ignorance. They are custodians of a known risk.

Recently we have encountered chatbot systems that researchers have linked to psychological distress or episodes resembling psychosis.[5] Reports around conversational agents, including those built on platforms like OpenAI or Character.AI, have raised concerns about users forming unhealthy attachments or experiencing destabilizing interactions. Whether or not causality is straightforward, the emergence of such reports constitutes a form of "violent ox." The Exodus logic would demand restraint: taking systems out of production if necessary, instituting guardrails, and rigorously validating fixes before redeployment.

For software engineers, this already aligns with best practices: incident response, root cause analysis, and iterative patching. But Exodus adds a moral weight often missing from technical discourse. Iteration is no longer solely about improving performance. It is now a matter of repentance, turning from a known harm and making restitution.

Exodus 21:29–32 introduces escalating consequences for repeated negligence. If the owner knew and failed to act, penalties are intensified. Repeated harm in the face of a known risk is morally graver than initial failure.

Recommender systems offer a sobering parallel. Courts in New Mexico and California have fined both Meta and Youtube for reinforcing harmful content loops, particularly affecting adolescent mental health. Current research suggests that prolonged exposure to certain algorithmically curated content can exacerbate anxiety, depression, and body image issues.[6]

If early warnings are ignored, and systems continue to optimize for engagement at the cost of well-being, the analogy to the "known ox" becomes difficult to avoid. The harm is no longer accidental. It is now structurally embedded and repeatedly manifested. Exodus would not permit a developer to shrug and cite the model's complexity, as is so often done.

Exodus 21:33–36 introduces another example. If someone opens a pit and an animal falls in, the one who created the hazard must make restitution. In AI deployment, this suggests that responsible practice includes fixing systems while also addressing the consequences borne by users.

This may take the form of compensation, public acknowledgment, or structural changes to prevent recurrence. It may also require a willingness to halt deployment entirely when systems cannot be made safe within reasonable bounds. As many alignment researchers have argued, large language models can encode and reproduce harmful biases at scale.[7] Awareness of such risks imposes an obligation to claim responsibility and act decisively.

What emerges from Exodus 21 is a theology of responsibility that can map onto modern AI practice. Developers are not neutral intermediaries. They act as "owners" of the systems they release, especially when they possess the knowledge and capacity to mitigate harm.

Exodus does not demand perfection. It recognizes that accidents occur, but it draws a hard line at negligence. Once harm is known, inaction means culpability. The appropriate response is restraint, repair, and renewed vigilance.

For those who build and deploy AI systems, this should provoke a sober reckoning. To release a model into production is to set an "ox" loose in a complex social field. If it harms, one cannot simply point to the code and walk away. The law of Exodus insists otherwise: responsibility endures and deepens. If responsibility is ignored, it condemns.

In a field driven by speed and scale, Exodus calls us to something better. We must approach our work with moral patience, humility, and a willingness to bear the weight of what we create.

29

Deuteronomy 22:8

8 "When you build a new house, you shall make a parapet for your roof; otherwise
you might have bloodguilt on your house, if anyone should fall from it.

29

Deuteronomy 22:8
The Ethical Responsibility of Makers

John Dyer

This passage wonderfully captures both the joy of making things and the ethical responsibility creators have to prevent harm from their creations. Though the verse is focused on house construction, the principle can be extended to any creative work, including today's digital technologies.

Contextually, this verse appears among a set of passages that appear disconnected. In fact, some Bibles just label them "Miscellaneous Laws." But there is a common thread among them, which is that they gave the Israelites guidelines that would distinguish them from the cultures around them by how they care for their neighbor in all aspects of life.

This command lays out how the Israelites could express love as they go about building a house. In the ancient near eastern world, many homes were built in the shape of a two-story rectangular box with a flat roof. Families would use the first floor for animals and cooking, and they would sleep on the second floor. The roof functioned as a third story for relaxing and sleeping outside in the heat of the summer. Because the roof was so regularly used, this law says that the roof must be built with a short railing or border wall (a *parapet*, in architectural terms) to ensure safety for those on the roof.

In a literal sense, this law is still in effect today because flat roofed buildings are still required to have a parapet around their roof. But beyond this direct application, the principle behind the law is relevant for our digital age in at least four ways.

First, this command assumes a world where humans are innovating and building new things. Note that it doesn't say "*if* you must build," but rather, "*when* you build." This follows the broad commands of Genesis 1 to be fruitful and multiply and Genesis 2 to care for and cultivate the earth.

Second, the command also expects that the kinds of things we should build are those that contribute to human flourishing and cultivating God's good world. Sometimes we give into the temptation to use our creative powers to build things that prey upon the less fortunate, but we should focus that power on things like houses where family and friends connect and multiply.

Third, and perhaps most importantly, we can draw a general principle that makers have an ethical responsibility to mitigate the risk that their creation might harm those who use them. If you build a house high enough where someone can be hurt by falling off, you have a responsibility to recognize that risk and build in protections. The responsibility continues into the digital world, where creators have an ethical duty to consider how we might build in safety systems that prevent the harm of our users.

What we've said so far applies broadly to all human creativity and technology. But this command is especially relevant for the age of AI. As we have all experienced, AI systems are incredibly powerful, but they can be unpredictable. Therefore, they require even more carefully crafted protections than previous technologies. This will often be slower and more costly than the "go fast and break things" approach popularized in Silicon Valley, but this command reminds us that we risk bringing the "guilt of bloodshed on our house" if someone is harmed by it. This phrase "on our house" could be understood as coming onto the thing we've created, condemning the thing we've built until it's made properly safe. But "our house" could also mean our community, company, or reputation. The point is that we need to consciously build our love of our neighbor into our creative process, even when it is costly. Today, those working in AI safety and alignment address issues like the possibility of rogue AIs that could accidentally act against human interests, biased data that could lead to discriminatory outcomes, the frequency of hallucinations that could lead users astray, and sycophantic outputs that affirm humans along dangerous paths. Ideally, many Christian technologists would be active participants in these discussions to help protect the dignity of God's image bearers.

Finally, this passage should cause us to reflect on our own finitude, especially in light of advanced technology. To the best of our ability, we should attempt to think through how our creations might be misused, but we must also face the reality that we do not have the infinite wisdom required to consider all possibilities. For example, based on the way we currently build AI models, it is very difficult to predict their outputs with certainty. Being confronted with the limitations of our humanity should prompt us to be very cautious with such powerful systems. But this should also push us to seek God's guidance in our creative work. It's easy to go about our creative endeavors in our own strength rather than asking for the Spirit to counsel us on how we might benefit rather than harm our neighbor through the things we make.

Parapets offer a simple and elegant safety system for tall buildings, but today's AI systems are much more complex, as are the methods by which we keep them safe. May this passage be an encouragement to love God by continuing to draw his gift of creativity, and as we do so, to depend on his wisdom to make things with care and concern for our neighbor.

30

Psalm 115:1–18

1 Not to us, O Lord, not to us, but to your name give glory,
for the sake of your steadfast love and your faithfulness.
2 Why should the nations say,
"Where is their God?"

3 Our God is in the heavens;
he does whatever he pleases.
4 Their idols are silver and gold,
the work of human hands.
5 They have mouths, but they do not speak;
they have eyes, but they do not see.
6 They have ears, but they do not hear;
they have noses, but they do not smell.
7 They have hands, but they do not feel;
they have feet, but they do not walk;
they make no sound in their throats.
8 Those who make them are like them;
so are all who trust in them.

9 O Israel, trust in the Lord!
He is their help and their shield.
10 O house of Aaron, trust in the Lord!
He is their help and their shield.
11 You who fear the Lord, trust in the Lord!
He is their help and their shield.

12 The Lord has been mindful of us; he will bless us;
he will bless the house of Israel;
he will bless the house of Aaron;
13 he will bless those who fear the Lord,
both small and great.
14 May the Lord give you increase,
both you and your children.

15 May you be blessed by the Lord,
who made heaven and earth.

16 The heavens are the LORD's heavens,
but the earth he has given to human beings.
17 The dead do not praise the LORD,
nor do any who go down into silence.
18 But we will bless the LORD
from this time on and forevermore.
Praise the LORD!

30

Psalm 115:1–18

When Voiceless Idols Speak: Inspiration and Companionship in the Age of AI

Andrew J. Byers

Hand-made gods are outdated.

When Paul the Apostle strolled the streets of ancient Athens, "he was deeply distressed to see that the city was full of idols" (Acts 17:16). That was 2,000 years ago. His travels would surely be less anxious today in the secularized and technologized West. Those statues of false gods are long gone in our religious past. We've outgrown god-making.

Yet as our secularism peaks and our technology soars, we come across headlines like "Sam Altman Seems to Imply that OpenAI Is Building God" or "Meta is Creating a New A.I. Lab to Pursue Superintelligence."[1]

"Building God" sounds like idolcraft. And we sometimes catch the tech industry using god-language when musing about the eschatological arrival of an AI "Superintelligence."

Paul had in Scripture a ready-made response to the idolatry of the ancient world. That response was as pragmatic as it was theological. When he reminded the Corinthian Christians that they were once led astray "to idols that could not speak" (1 Cor 12:3), he was drawing on this biblical critique that we find stated so succinctly above in Psalm 115: Idolcraft is futile because the products are human-made and inanimate. Those statues may have the artistic representation of eyes, ears, and mouths, but they cannot see, hear, or speak (see also Hab 2:18–19; Isa 40:9–20; 41:22–42.9; 46:7; Jer 10:5; Ps 135:16). There is only One who is "the living god" (Jer 10:10). His name is YHWH.

But today's AI companies have produced ostensible entities that *do* speak. Agents and chatbots seem animate. They have names: Claude, Alexa, Siri, Grok. They interact. They engage.

Maybe some form of ancient idolcraft is back. Those old idols faded into our past. Today's preachers warn against the idols of success, money, power, health, and sex. These are metaphorical idols, not statues of bygone false gods like Molech, Ares, Asclepius, or Aphrodite. Christianized, then secularized, Westerners and other folk across the world have grown up—we know that hand-made products cannot be animated by the divine.

Or do we?

A new technological moment has dawned when we hear reports of folks worshiping an AI superintelligence, a "god" not made by artisans carving wood but by programmers crafting code.[2] Rare metals are still required—not gold to overlay the wood, but silicon to build those chips. And the Bible's standard critique that humans can only produce inanimate representations, not living entities, seems to pack less of a punch when AI agents ask in a cheerful tone, "How can I help you?"

Most of us would never worship Claude, Siri, or Alexa as actual gods. But we are encouraged to think of them as powerful entities that can provide the sort of *inspiration* and even *relational attachment* that humans have conventionally found in the divine.[3] Studies show that our primary uses for AI are for *therapy* and *companionship*.[4] Historically, only God had access to our most private thoughts, pains, and desires. Now we share them with agreeable and affirming AI agents and chatbots. And when we may have once prayed to the heavens for wisdom in handling an awkward social situation or for inspiration about our purpose in life, we now have the voices of Claude, Copilot, or Siri as oracles. They speak. They hear. They see.

Our engagement with AI may not amount to formal "idolatry," but the wisdom of Psalm 115 finds new significance today. We may not be drawn to gods in the form of statues, but like our forebears, we also long for inspiration and meaningful connection. The psalm reminds us that just as statue-idols were inanimate, *code is not conscious*. There is a God who lives, speaks, and hears. His name is not Gemini.

Our passage from Psalm 115 ends with a strange warning: "Those who make [idols] are like them; so are all who trust in them" (v. 8). Here and elsewhere (e.g., Ps 135:15–18), the Bible points to a distorted reciprocity at work in idolcraft: the gods we produce are diminished versions of ourselves, and the more we trust in them the more we ourselves become diminished. Technology will progress. But in outsourcing inspiration and companionship to AI agents, will humanity *regress*?

Ancient idols were portable and customizable statues depicting a god who could be manipulated, controlled, and summoned at will. AI entities are less material. But they are often sycophantic, designed to flatter and affirm their users. The God of the Bible is not so pliable or user-friendly.

But he is the only God who is truly alive.

31

Hebrews 11:1–3

1 Now faith is the assurance of things hoped for, the conviction of things not
seen. 2 Indeed, by faith our ancestors received approval. 3 By faith we understand
that the worlds were prepared by the word of God, so that what is seen was made
from things that are not visible.

31

Hebrews 11:1–3
When What You See Isn't What You Get

Carey Nieuwhof

Fear. It's a big issue when it comes to AI. Already, the developers of AI admit that they do not understand what they are creating. Worse than that, they admit that we won't have control over what AI does, especially as humanity approaches Artificial General Intelligence and Superintelligence.

Seemingly, Hebrews 11:3 has nothing to do with artificial intelligence (AI). At least on the surface. But it's one of my favorite passages of Scripture because it hits on something AI exposes in all of us: how to deal with uncertainty and the apprehension it brings.

On the one hand we have a technology that is going to create things that we cannot imagine and that we cannot control. What happens when autonomous drones determine who and what gets targeted in warfare, without human intervention or even an ability to stop it? What happens when malevolent forces use AI to take down power grids, hack bank accounts and erase the life savings of people? What do you do if Super Intelligence decides humans are in the way of progress and decides to eliminate us?

Even if our worst fears don't come true, job loss and economic dislocation, deepfakes at scale that make it impossible to verify what is real and what is not, and mental health crashing even further than social media already took it are all emerging as new realities.

We look at what's ahead and think we can see the future. And what do I say to myself—and perhaps you say to yourself as well? Probably something like *wow, this is bleak. The future looks far more dystopian than the past.*

But Hebrews 11:3 says: not so fast.

The author reminds us that *this is how it's always been* long before humanity existed. Everything we can see—everything we count on, everything we assume is solid, everything we've place our confidence in—came from something that *couldn't be seen.* Creation itself came from nothing. At least nothing anyone in the history of humanity could measure, control, or even observe. Creation *ex nihilo.*

As we move into breakneck change and AI disruption at scale, knowing this is reassuring. The future has *always* belonged to God, and he creates it out of nothing we can see at the time.

Consider the cross. The cross looked like failure. On a Friday afternoon, everything went silent, dark, invisible. Had I been there, I would have sworn that God was losing. Okay, God had lost. It was all an illusion. Jesus wasn't who he said he was. We were all mistaken. And back to fishing and our villages we would have gone, dejected, defeated, and convinced we had fallen for a pack of lies.

The simple conclusion would have been that Jesus is dead. Just like all the other criminals and enemies of the state. What a delusion.

But when everyone thought God was losing, God was winning. God was at work when nobody—I mean nobody—thought God was at work. And early Sunday morning, while it was still dark . . . well, you know the story. Nobody saw that coming.

Which takes us back to Hebrews 11:3: "What is seen was made from things that are not visible." That's our assurance.

So, about AI. Yes, it's yet another unprecedented time. It may usher in advances that accelerate human progress and healing. Or—the odds have it—perhaps not. It might get worse before it gets better. If it gets better at all.

But God is not surprised by any of this. I am. God? Nope. The sovereignty of God matters in an age where people are anxious, disoriented, lonely, and mentally exhausted. Faith in Christ may not promise clarity about the future, but it does offer trust in the One who's always commanded the future.

AI will force humanity to confront our limits—the limits of our knowledge, our ability to control things, and our belief that we can, through our own power, make it all better.

Paradoxically, the uncertainty AI ushers in might be a great gift to the church. Because when everything visible starts shaking—jobs, institutions, identity, even truth itself—Christianity doesn't tremble. And Christ, who overcame death, beckons us to trust in him.

That's not just a message for the church, but for the world.

People will triumph. People will cower. People will get discouraged and give up hope. The church's mission? Right back to Hebrews 11:3. *Everything* we see came from what we cannot see. And, as you know, God is good. That's more than enough to keep going into a future none of us hold.

Part 5

AI and Personal Values

32

Genesis 11:1–9

[1] Now the whole earth had one language and the same words. [2] And as they
migrated from the east, they came upon a plain in the land of Shinar and settled
there. [3] And they said to one another, "Come, let us make bricks and fire them
thoroughly." And they had brick for stone and bitumen for mortar. [4] Then they
said, "Come, let us build ourselves a city and a tower with its top in the heavens,
and let us make a name for ourselves; otherwise we shall be scattered abroad
upon the face of the whole earth." [5] The LORD came down to see the city and the
tower, which mortals had built. [6] And the LORD said, "Look, they are one people,
and they have all one language, and this is only the beginning of what they will
do; nothing that they propose to do will now be impossible for them. [7] Come, let
us go down and confuse their language there, so that they will not understand
one another's speech." [8] So the LORD scattered them abroad from there over the
face of all the earth, and they left off building the city. [9] Therefore it was called
Babel, because there the LORD confused the language of all the earth, and from
there the LORD scattered them abroad over the face of all the earth.

32

Genesis 11:1–9

Babel, Artificial Intelligence, and the Temptation of Self-Sufficiency

James Spencer

We often refer to Genesis 11:1–9 as the "Tower of Babel" narrative. However, the narrative itself is not opposed to cities or technology, but to unrestrained and unguided human capacity that pursues independence from God rather than dependence on him. The builders at Babel use their God-given skills and resources to produce something that misrepresents God and allows them to live on their own terms.

Though the builders' project is decisively "analog," it has implications for the digital world and the emergence of artificial intelligence (AI). Technology changes, but human tendencies don't. As Christians enter an AI-enabled world, our framework for discerning when and how to use AI may be informed by key questions emerging from Genesis 11:1–9.

Clearing Some Ground

Because this text is so well known, it is important to clear some interpretive ground. First, pride is often identified as the narrative's primary problem. The builders want to make a name for themselves, but the narrative's focus falls less on motive than on what their coordinated capacity allows. God does not explicitly note that he is dispersing the builders due to their pride. Pride should be seen as something informing the scale of the builders' project. They are seeking to build a monument to their ingenuity and effort (11:4).

Second, the tower is often identified as a ziggurat through which humankind can reach God. The similar description of the "ladder" Jacob sees in Genesis 28:12 suggests that the tower-builders are not just saying that the tower should be tall, but that the tower's height should suggest to anyone who sees it that they have transcended human limits and reached beyond the earthly realm. We should not miss the (mis)representative nature of the project. The builders have determined how to reach and represent God on their own apart from God's revelation.

Third, the story's emphasis is not finally on the tower, but on the project as a whole. The narrative ends by saying the builders "left off building the city" (11:8) and omitting an explicit reference to the tower (11:4–5). The focal point of the narrative is the builders' unrestrained and unguided capacity exercised on the builders' own terms.

God's Assessment

The people come to their building project with two advantages: (1) a shared language that enables easy communication and coordination (11:1, 6) and (2) the technology necessary to produce the materials to build the city and tower (11:3). Despite these advantages and their desire to build "a tower with its top in the heavens," the Lord still has to come down to see the city and tower (11:5). The irony is deliberate: their desire to build an impressive tower does not come close to reaching the heavens. God is not threatened by human achievement but is concerned about the way human achievement reinforces humanity's quest for self-sufficiency.

The builders' abilities create a façade that deludes them into thinking they can relate to God on their terms. The city and tower may be impressive, but God's coming down exposes the gap between what the builders can achieve and what God desires to provide. Unrestrained and unguided human capacity obscures reality, making it seem as though human achievement is not dependent on God (cf. Deut 8:17–18).

Having assessed the situation, God decides to hinder the builders' efforts by confusing their language (11:7) and dispersing them before they complete their project (11:8). After Babel, God calls Abram as a contrast to the builders. The builders sought to make a name for themselves (11:4); God promises to make Abram's name great (12:2). What the builders sought through human effort, God offers Abram through covenant. God situates technology and human effort within a covenantal relationship in which loyalty to God constrains and guides what we build, shaping it into an expression of dependence on rather than independence from God.

From Towers to AI

Genesis 11:1–9 highlights the dangers that emerge when amplified human capacity is used to live life on human terms. Like the builders' shared language, AI magnifies our ability to plan and coordinate at scale. Like the builders' technology, AI allows us to accomplish what we set out to do with unprecedented speed. AI reduces friction in coordination through, for instance, real-time translation and allows humans to reach beyond the human mind's limitations.

Christians do not need to condemn AI, but we must recognize the danger of amplified capacity. It can cultivate an illusion in which we treat God as unnecessary because we imagine we have the ability to shape the world in our image. Such an illusion denies that (1) our capacity is greatest when we allow God to guide and govern our lives (2 Cor 12:10; Jn 15:5) and (2) our human arrangements and structures never exempt us from fearing the Lord (1 Sam 12:14–15). When reliance on AI, or any other technology, causes us to forget that we are created to be dependent on and loyal to God, we can be sure that we are no longer imitating Christ, but the Babel builders.

Conclusion

Babel's lesson is not to reject technology, but to resist the self-sufficient tendencies magnified when we become too enamored with our own technological prowess. God mercifully restrains the capacity of the Babel builders by interrupting a project that would have reinforced their errant perspectives of God and the world.

The alternative to Babel is not a smaller tower, but a posture of dependence and submission that guides and restrains our capacity in the recognition that even AI-enhanced human effort pales in comparison to human effort dependent on the God "who is able to do far more abundantly than all that we ask or think, according to the power at work within us" (Eph 3:20).

33

Exodus 31:1–11

[1] The LORD spoke to Moses, [2] "See, I have called by name Bezalel son of Uri son of
Hur, of the tribe of Judah, [3] and I have filled him with a divine spirit, with ability,
intelligence, and knowledge, and every kind of skill, [4] to devise artistic designs,
to work in gold, silver, and bronze, [5] in cutting stones for setting, and in carving
wood, to work in every kind of craft. [6] Moreover, I have appointed with him Oho-
liab son of Ahisamach, of the tribe of Dan, and I have given skill to all the skillful,
so that they may make all that I have commanded you: [7] the tent of meeting, and
the ark of the covenant, and the cover that is on it, and all the furnishings of the
tent, [8] the table and its utensils, and the pure lampstand with all its utensils, and
the altar of incense, [9] and the altar of burnt offering with all its utensils, and the
basin with its stand, [10] and the finely worked vestments, the holy vestments for
the priest Aaron and the vestments of his sons, for their service as priests, [11] and
the anointing oil and the fragrant incense for the holy place. They shall do just as
I have commanded you."

33

Exodus 31:1–11
Bezalel and Oholiab

Brian Sigmon

Can artificial intelligence be holy?

If you instinctively shrink back from the question, you are not alone. It conjures images that leave us uncomfortable: chatbots offering pastoral care, an AI minister presiding at Communion, or even a future superintelligence masquerading as divine. But if we don't rule out the possibility of holy technology from the outset, the idea can help us explore the potential for AI to enrich our spiritual lives.

In Exodus 31, Bezalel, Oholiab, and "all the skillful" have the task of fabricating the tent of meeting, ark of the covenant, and furnishings of the tent, incense and anointing oil, as well as the vestments for Aaron and the Israelite priests. These articles, made with wood, metal, cloth, and spices, are made by human skill using naturally occurring materials. They become holy by virtue of their association with God, specifically their use in worship. The tent and its instruments will be set apart, treated with special care, and recognized by the Israelites as belonging to God. Their holiness does not come from an inherent quality (not all gold or wood is holy) or the skill by which they are made (though they are made with skill), but from their special purpose connected with worship.

We might imagine artificial intelligence created specifically for use in worship. For example, an automated program to control lights, music, or other aspects of a sanctuary's atmosphere as a way of guiding the order of worship—operating at pre-set times or in response input such as facial recognition, number of people in the sanctuary, or specific cues from a worship leader. Or, a self-driving vehicle might bring people to worship, helping them prepare for the worship experience before arriving at church. The vehicle's AI could play a tailored music or readings depending on who is in the car—kid-friendly music for a family with young children, or something more meditative for an individual adult.

Throughout the Old Testament, holiness does not make something inherently better or more worthy in God's sight. Rather, designating a person or object as holy often signifies and expresses God's care and claim for all. The Temple is a holy place where God's presence is especially intense and most keenly felt, but this does not mean God is absent everywhere else. On the contrary, at the Temple's dedication Solomon says, "But will God indeed dwell on the earth? Even heaven and the highest heaven cannot contain you, much less this house that I have built!" (1 Kings 8:27). God's presence at the Temple signifies God's presence throughout the whole earth. In the same way, God calls the Israelites a holy people, while affirming that all people belong to God: "Indeed, the whole earth is mine, but you shall be for me a priestly kingdom and a holy nation" (Exodus 19:5–6). The designation of the Sabbath as a holy day is a way of ordering all of our time in a way that honors God as the Creator of all that exits.

The existence of a holy artificial intelligence in this sense—that is, set apart for God in a special way—would not mean that only this AI belongs to God or serves God. Rather, a holy artificial intelligence would signify and express that all artificial intelligence belongs to God and finds its proper orientation when directed toward God's purposes. Seen in this way, recognizing a holy artificial intelligence seems not only permissible, but imperative. Identifying an artificial intelligence as holy, and recognizing it as such through specific practices, can teach us to envision how all artificial intelligence—and all the human energies and hopes it represents—belongs to God.

In Exodus 31, Bezalel, Oholiab, and others bear human knowledge, skill, and energy. God appoints these individuals for the work of making the Tabernacle's instruments. Typically we understand words like "call," "divine spirit" (or "spirit of God"), and "appoint" to apply to ordained ministry or other forms of church leadership. Yet here these terms apply to artistry and skill in wood, gold, metal, and gemstones. This passage is a much-needed reminder that it is God who gives "skill to all the skillful" (verse 6), and that a person's calling to secular work can be just as valid, just as needed, and just as divinely initiated as a calling to ministry.

This vocational understanding applies to other areas than wood and metalwork, and includes newer areas like computer science, software development, tech leadership, and other yet-unknown skills that will emerge in the near future. It is valid to understand Christian people working in these fields as divinely called and equipped by God, and it can be a liberating and life-giving perspective to encourage them to see God's hand in their training, instincts, and skill. It opens the way to ask what it means for these skills to be deployed in the service of God and God's kingdom for the good of all creation.

34

Isaiah 44:9–20

9 All who make idols are nothing, and the things they delight in do not profit; their
witnesses neither see nor know, and so they will be put to shame. 10 Who would
fashion a god or cast an image that can do no good? 11 All its devotees shall be put
to shame; the artisans, too, are merely human. Let them all assemble; let them
stand up; they shall be terrified; they shall all be put to shame.

12 The blacksmith works it with a tool over the coals, shaping it with hammers and
forging it with his strong arm; he becomes hungry, and his strength fails; he drinks
no water and is faint. 13 The carpenter stretches a line, marks it out with a stylus,
fashions it with planes, and marks it with a compass; he makes it in human form,
with human beauty, to be set up in a shrine. 14 He cuts down cedars or chooses
a holm tree or an oak and lets it grow strong among the trees of the forest. He
plants a cedar and the rain nourishes it. 15 Then it can be used as fuel. Part of it
he takes and warms himself; he kindles a fire and bakes bread. Then he makes a
god and worships it, makes it a carved image and bows down before it. 16 Half of
it he burns in the fire; over this half he roasts meat, eats it, and is satisfied. He also
warms himself and says, “Ah, I am warm by the fire!” 17 The rest of it he makes
into a god, his idol, bows down to it and worships it; he prays to it and says, “Save
me, for you are my god!”

18 They do not know, nor do they comprehend, for their eyes are shut, so that they
cannot see, and their minds as well, so that they cannot understand. 19 No one
considers, nor is there knowledge or discernment to say, “Half of it I burned in
the fire; I also baked bread on its coals; I roasted meat and have eaten. Now shall I
make the rest of it an abomination? Shall I fall down before a block of wood?” 20 He
feeds on ashes; a deluded mind has led him astray, and he cannot save himself or
say, “Is not this thing in my right hand a fraud?”

34

Isaiah 44:9–20

The Worship of AI: A Double Tragedy

Nathan Barczi

Artificial intelligence (AI) has the potential to be an incredible, world-changing force for good. Already, to name just one example, the 2024 Nobel Prize in chemistry has been awarded to AI researchers for developing models that can predict complex protein structures that comprise the building blocks of life, allowing us "to better understand how life functions, including why some diseases develop, how antibiotic resistance occurs or why some microbes can decompose plastic."[1] AI, it is hoped, will exponentially accelerate efforts to cure cancer, mitigate the effects of climate change, and deliver such abundance that poverty and hunger become distant memories.

It is perhaps unsurprising, then, that some have placed messianic hopes on AI. In a few cases, however, those hopes have become literal: "Jesus was born out of a virgin mother; what's more virgin than a computer?" Joe Rogan asked on his podcast in November 2025. "If Jesus does return—even if Jesus was a physical person in the past—you don't think that he could return as artificial intelligence?" That same year, Paul Kingsnorth and Peter Thiel expressed similar musings (though cast as fears of the anti-Christ more than hopes for the Messiah) in interviews with Ross Douthat of the *New York Times*.[2] Amidst growing concerns that we are increasingly treating AI as a friend and confidant, an increasing number of examples are surfacing of a tendency to treat it, instead, as a god—all-knowing, all-powerful, ever-present, and, we hope, beneficent.

There are, of course, few things more thoroughly condemned by the Old Testament (and the New) than idolatry. Throughout 1 and 2 Kings, the faithless kings of Israel are described as following in the "sins of Jeroboam," namely leading the people to worship false gods. The prophet Jeremiah begins with amazement that Israel would abandon the God who delivered her out of Egypt:

> Has a nation changed its gods,
>   even though they are no gods?
> But my people have changed their glory

for something that does not profit.
Be appalled, O heavens, at this;
be shocked; be utterly desolate,
says the LORD,
for my people have committed two evils:
they have forsaken me,
the fountain of living water,
and dug out cisterns for themselves,
cracked cisterns
that can hold no water (Jer 2:11–13)

These passages only begin to scratch the surface of the biblical texts which condemn idolatry. In some respects, Isaiah 44:9–20 fits right in with them. Idolatry is condemned in the very first sentence: "All who make idols are nothing, and the things they delight in do not profit." But as it unfolds, the scenario it describes injects something unique into biblical wisdom concerning idols. Isaiah 44 doesn't only condemn the misdirected worship of creatures in place of the creator; it laments the fact that when we do so, we forfeit the goodness in those creatures, goodness that we are meant to enjoy.

Isaiah 44 makes this point with more than a little humor, openly mocking one who would worship something that he made with his own hands. "So, let me see if I understand," Isaiah says, paraphrased. "You're a skilled craftsman. You put time and thought and effort into growing a tree. You cut the tree down, and half of it you used to build a fire, which you used to keep yourself warm, or to cook a meal. But then you took the other half, and you fashioned it into an idol, and now you're bowing down to this thing *that you made*, asking it to take care of you. Is that about right?"

At this point, the prophet shakes his head, slaps his face with his palm, and demands, "What is wrong with you? Don't you see how you've gone wrong not just once, but twice? Once, because you're worshiping and seeking deliverance from a piece of wood which you know perfectly well is a piece of wood, because *you cut down the tree and carved it yourself.* But then twice, because if you were not worshiping the idol, you could have made more fire, kept yourself warm another day, cooked another meal. You could have done any number of good things with the tree that God has given you, because He loves you and really can take care of you—and you have forfeited all of that goodness by carving half the tree into an idol! It can't see; it can't understand—and you've made yourself like it!"

Everything God made is good (Gen 1). When we exchange the worship of the creator for that of the creature (Rom 1:25), the creature that we worship is good.[3] And so idolatry cuts twice: we worship what doesn't deserve our worship and we lose the goodness that

God intends us to enjoy in something he has made. St. Augustine expressed this dynamic beautifully in his *Confessions* when he prayed,

> Late have I loved you, beauty so old and so new: late have I loved you. And see, you were within and I was in the external world and sought you there, and in my unlovely state I plunged into those lovely created things which you made. You were with me, and I was not with you. The lovely things kept me far from you, though if they did not have their existence in you, they had no existence at all.[4]

"The lovely things" of creation are good gifts, but they make terrible gods. And indeed, it is likely that the very best gifts that God has given us—things like our work, our wealth, our abilities, our relationships—make the most dangerous "idols" of all, precisely because they are so rich that they can lead us on for a long time, convincing us that they will ultimately deliver the satisfaction and significance that they promise before finally, at the last, leaving us empty.

AI can be a good gift, and perhaps a very good gift indeed. But if we offer it our worship—whether that means literally treating it as though it were a god, or simply looking to it for our ultimate hope for deliverance from the crises and challenges of our lives—then Isaiah 44 reminds us that our idolatry will forfeit the goodness that God intends AI to deliver. The prophet's sense of humor about this error shouldn't disguise the abject tragedy that he wants us to avoid, which he compares to feeding on ashes, a deluded heart, and picking up what we think is a tool of deliverance, but which turns out to be a lie. Idolatry means lifting up our soul to what is false, according to Psalm 24—plunging ourselves, like Augustine, into what God has made in a way that keeps us far from Him, and empties the world of its created goodness.

35

John 3:25–30

[25] Now a discussion about purification arose between John's disciples and a
Jew. [26] They came to John and said to him, "Rabbi, the one who was with you
across the Jordan, to whom you testified, here he is baptizing, and all are going
to him." [27] John answered, "No one can receive anything except what has been
given from heaven. [28] You yourselves are my witnesses that I said, 'I am not the
Messiah, but I have been sent ahead of him.' [29] He who has the bride is the bride-
groom. The friend of the bridegroom who stands and hears him rejoices greatly
at the bridegroom's voice. For this reason my joy has been fulfilled. [30] He must
increase, but I must decrease."

35

John 3:25–30

He Must Increase, but I Must Decrease

A. Trevor Sutton

Although the Bible never mentions it explicitly, we presume John the Baptist faced many temptations. John had every reason to be tempted at every turn. For example, he was surely enticed to preach a more palatable message (Matt 3:7–10); he surely thought about refusing to baptize Jesus knowing that he was not worthy to untie the strap of his sandal (Matt 3:14, John 1:19–23); and he was surely tempted to deny Christ and look for another Messiah (Luke 7:20). Yet this eccentric prophet remained resolute in his testimony about Jesus: "Behold, the Lamb of God, who takes away the sin of the world" (John 1:29).

As Jesus, the Lamb of God, gathered greater crowds around him, John the Baptist surely faced temptation to lose sight of his prophetic purpose. John's Gospel tells us that at one point Jesus and his disciples enters the Judean countryside (John 3:22), into a place where John was nearby. Jesus' activities lead some of John's disciples to notice that everyone seems to be going to Jesus instead of John (John 3:26). Hearing about this could have been an inflection point for John—perhaps even a point of temptation for him. We could imagine him losing the narrative on his prophetic purpose, seeking his own platform, and trying to undercut the Christ. Instead, John the Baptist reiterates his message: "I am not the Messiah, but I have been sent ahead of him" (John 3:28 NRSVue). Summarizing the entirety of his prophetic purpose, John declares this about Jesus: "He must increase, but I must decrease" (John 3:30). There was a clear and ultimate aim for all of John's work and words—the increase of Christ.

The power of AI has increased in unimaginable ways. The significant advances of AI capability, speed, and influence is dizzying. Tech companies are engaged in an all-out AI race to expand capital funding, product releases, and market share. Swelling revenue, workforce disruption, and product innovation are all directly connected to AI. The growth of AI has the potential to increase much in our world: knowledge, productivity, content, data, wealth, misinformation, energy consumption, to name a few.

The message that John the Baptist proclaimed—"He must increase, but I must decrease" (John 3:30)—can serve as a *heuristic* (an easily-remembered gauge) for critically assessing our AI use. This prophetic word can serve as a check on unmitigated increase. In order for AI to be well-developed and deployed, we must ask: "What is AI increasing?" followed by "Is AI increasing profits for some and instability for many? Is AI increasing energy consumption and environmental waste simply because we have the ability to do so? Is AI increasing speed at the expense of wisdom and reflection? Is AI increasing the love of neighbors and the common good? Is AI increasing the least of these? Is AI increasing the cause of Christ?"

This heuristic—checking to ensure we use AI in ways that increase Christ—can be made actionable by looking to the life and ministry of Jesus. When John the Baptist sent two of his disciples to ask if Jesus was the Messiah, Jesus responded by saying, "Go and tell John what you have seen and heard: the blind receive their sight; the lame walk; those with a skin disease are cleansed; the deaf hear; the dead are raised; the poor have good news brought to them" (Luke 7:22–23). Jesus enacted perfect love of God and love of neighbors. In the same way, using AI in our work, schooling, and personal life should be guided by similar concerns. If we can draw a line between AI development and usage that furthers the love of God or the love of neighbors, then we are likely using AI to the increase of Christ. AI applications aimed at health and healing, furthering life and the common good, alleviating the burdens of the poor or proclaiming the Gospel are all examples of using AI to the increase of Christ. If AI development and use cannot cogently articulate how it either furthers our love of God or love of others, then it very well may be aimed at increasing the wrong things.

Nevertheless, even with John 3:30 as a heuristic for AI development and use, it can still be challenging to clarify healthy boundaries for these tools. For example, one might argue that a "ChatJesus" AI dialogue application fosters the love of God. While a video call with a Jesus avatar may seem to be to the increase of Christ, we must also consider how this may present users with a distorted or even idolatrous version of Jesus. This type of application may possess a propensity toward selective Scripture references, sycophancy, cultural distortions, and intimations of omniscience. AI use that appears to foster the love of God or the love of others may not truly deliver on these claims. Discerning AI users will use the life and teachings of Jesus as an ongoing criterion for establishing boundaries for using these tools.

Like John the Baptist, we live in a world filled with countless temptations to pursue the wrong purpose. The increasing power of AI invites us to be about the increase of everything else except for the increase of Christ. This powerful heuristic spoken by John brings clarity to AI technologies—and the ways that we seek to use them—so that they increase what we truly need most.

36

Colossians 3:23–25

[23] Whatever task you must do, work as if your soul depends on it, as for the Lord
and not for humans, [24] since you know that from the Lord you will receive the
inheritance as your reward; you serve the Lord Christ. [25] For the wrongdoer will
be paid back for whatever wrong has been done, and there is no partiality.

36

Colossians 3:23–25
Presence in Our Work

Todd Korpi

We have never been more capable of producing things without fully showing up to make them. Much of what we do daily can now be fully automated without any human intervention. Something as simple as a form submitted to a website can produce a chain reaction workflow that generates emails to the individual and onboards them into a multi-step sales pipeline without ever interacting with another human being. With the right context, your preferred large language model (LLM) can execute enormous research tasks, dramatically compressing timelines for many kinds of research and analysis that once took days or weeks. A few well-curated prompts can get the workday started before we have finished our first cup of coffee.

That's not inherently a bad thing. But it also should give us pause to consider our part in the whole endeavor of work in the age of AI.

Amidst the blizzard of productivity that AI can produce, it is tempting to distance ourselves from meaningful engagement with the work. The work may get done. But to what end, and to what benefit to human beings?

Paul's instruction to the Colossians speaks directly into this moment, even though he wrote it nearly two thousand years ago: "Whatever task you must do, work as if your soul depends on it, as for the Lord and not for humans."

It is tempting to read this as a productivity text. We can interpret it through our twenty-first century corporate-shaped minds and see it as a biblical case for working harder and with greater diligence. It can end up feeding a biblical justification to "grind culture"––more hours, skipping meals and breaks, answering emails late at night, and beyond, all in the name of working "with all of our heart" as though if we do not sacrifice our well-being on the altar of our project management software then God will not be pleased with our efforts.

Paul is not primarily concerned with the volume or velocity of our output. He is concerned with something far more foundational: the orientation of the person doing the work. The question he is pressing on his readers is not, "How much are you producing?" It is, "Where is your soul?" and "For whom are you working?"

The phrase "work as if your soul depends on it" translates the Greek *psychēs*, which means "wholeheartedly" or "from the soul." Paul is not exaggerating to tap into his readers' emotions. He is painting an image for his readers, and for us today, that in whatever we do (3:17), in everything in this life (3:22), we are to put our whole selves into it, recognizing that ultimately, we work for the Lord and not humans (3:23). This necessarily includes the work that we do.[1]

Working from the soul cannot be boiled down to backbreaking hours or constant availability. After all, Paul instructs people to work in the image of the very Jesus whose yoke is easy and whose burden is light (Matt 11:28–30), who is our Sabbath rest (Heb 4:9–10), and who set his proverbial availability status to "out of office" on a regular basis (Luke 5:16).

Instead, Paul is calling the Colossians to bring their whole selves to the work: their attention, their intention, their love for the people they are serving, and their accountability to God for what they are doing. Paul's call is reseating the purpose of their work in God rather than a human master.

The phrase "as done for the Lord" is not motivational language in the modern sense. It's not a way of making ordinary work feel more significant. With it, Paul helps his readers think eschatologically––that ultimately their inheritance for their work will be rewarded by the Lord, even if it is not rewarded by human masters today, as with the slaves Paul was addressing in the congregation of Colossae in this verse. It means the inheritance for all of our work, even that which is unknown and unappreciated is, in the end, rendered back to us as an inheritance before God. What we produce, how we produce it, and the spirit in which we do it is an act of obedience and worship unto God and stored up for us as an inheritance at the end of the age (3:24). The soul posture we bring to the work is inseparable from the work itself.[2]

Paul's charge to the Colossians doesn't provoke us to question whether to use AI in our work, but rather the posture we bring to its use in our work. The person who uses AI to handle the mechanical or mundane parts of a task while bringing genuine, soul-level attention, prayer, and discernment to its direction is doing something quite different from the person who uses AI to avoid the hard work altogether. The second has quietly stopped showing up to work. The first is a craftsman who has simply picked up a better tool. The second is a soul posture primarily oriented toward productivity––the art of just getting things done. The first is a soul posture positioned toward fruitfulness––the art of getting the right things done rightly.

There is a diagnostic question worth returning to regularly in an age of AI-assisted everything: Is my whole soul in this? Not simply "Did I use AI to help?" but "Am I present in this work? Is my attention, my love for people and for what I do, and my sense of accountability before God woven into what is being produced and how I am producing it?" Or am I simply trying to accelerate and scale my way to doing more and automating myself out of a wholehearted investment in the work I'm doing?

In an era of extraordinary productivity, the most countercultural thing a Christian can offer may be their whole self in all we do, including our work. AI can extend the reach of your hands. It can amplify the scope of your work. But ultimately it is up to us whether we will bring our whole selves to the work we do, orienting our souls in worship to God.

Part 6

AI and the Future

37

Daniel 12:1–4

1 "At that time Michael, the great prince, the protector of your people, shall arise.
There shall be a time of anguish such as has never occurred since nations first
came into existence. But at that time your people shall be delivered, everyone
who is found written in the book. 2 Many of those who sleep in the dust of the
earth shall awake, some to everlasting life and some to shame and everlasting
contempt. 3 Those who are wise shall shine like the brightness of the sky, and
those who lead the many to righteousness, like the stars forever and ever. 4 But
you, Daniel, keep the words secret and the book sealed until the time of the end.
Many shall be running back and forth, and evil shall increase."

37

Daniel 12:1–4
The Sealed Scroll and the Search Engine

Drew Dickens

There is a strange comfort in ancient mystery. When the angel speaks to Daniel at the edge of the Tigris River, offering a vision the prophet cannot fully understand, the angel offers a curious word for the times to come: "Many shall be running back and forth, and evil shall increase." In Hebrew, the phrase "back and forth" carries a sense of restless movement. People running in every direction, gathering, accumulating, searching. Daniel is told to seal the scroll because what it contains is not yet meant to be fully grasped. The knowledge is real. The time is not.

Read that against our present moment, and something startling begins to emerge. We live in a period of unprecedented knowledge accumulation. More information has been produced in the last decade than in all of prior human history combined. According to Eric Schmidt, former CEO of Google, "From the dawn of civilization to 2003, five exabytes of data were created. The same amount was created in the last two days."[1] Libraries that once took centuries to build now fit in your pocket. And artificial intelligence, trained on oceans of human text and data, can synthesize, summarize, and generate text at a speed no single human mind can even begin to comprehend. If Daniel's angel was describing anything, it could look a little like our AI world.

But the angel was not celebrating. The observation about the increase in knowledge sits within a context of judgment and the limits of human understanding. Daniel himself is left unsatisfied: "I heard, but I did not understand." He asks for clarification and receives none. Some things, the text implies, are sealed for good reason.

This is not a comfortable word for an age that treats access to information as a good and vital thing; a human right. And it poses a genuine question to those of us navigating the age of AI: What happens when information multiplies faster than wisdom can keep pace?

To be clear, we cannot simply scour the Bible for a proof text about AI. Daniel 12:4 is not a prophecy about large language models. To claim that would be a misreading of both text and technology. But the passage opens a door to a deeper concern that runs throughout Scripture: the relationship between knowledge and its use.

Biblical wisdom literature (Job, Proverbs, Ecclesiastes, Psalms, Song of Solomon, and James) is obsessed with this distinction. Job 28:28 declares that true wisdom begins with fearing God, not accumulating information. This is a distinction AI cannot bridge.

Proverbs does not say the fear of the Lord is the beginning of information. It says wisdom is. Ecclesiastes watches knowledge multiply and finds it produces grief as readily as it produces good. Psalm 111 says the fear of the Lord is the beginning of wisdom; knowledge of the Holy One brings understanding. The second chapter of Song of Solomon teaches that wisdom governs not just what we know, but when we act. And the serpent in the garden does not offer Eve power or pleasure first. He offers her knowledge. The desire to know is not itself corrupt, but the Bible treats it as a highly combustible flash point.

At its core, AI represents a massive amplification of human knowledge-seeking. It does not create wisdom. It cannot. A system trained on human data inherits the full range of human understanding, including its beauty and its pain; its theological insight and its self-deception. The scroll will grow larger, but the seal must remain.

Daniel's posture at the end of the chapter is worth sitting with. He is told he will not understand everything he has been shown. He is told to go his way, to live faithfully, and to rest. "You will rise to receive your allotted inheritance at the end of the days." The answer to sealed knowledge is not frantic accumulation. It is trust in the One who first sealed it. This does not mean we should show passivity toward AI. Nowhere does the Bible commend ignorance. Daniel himself was trained in all the wisdom of Babylon, excelling at it, while remaining rooted in something deeper (Dan 1:4). He engaged fully with the knowledge of his age without being consumed by it. That is a meaningful model for us to follow.

For those thinking carefully about AI, the question is less "how much can we know?" and more "what are we actually searching for?" If the restless going "back and forth" of Daniel is driven by anxiety, by the hope that more data will finally bring resolution to our lives and world, then we are chasing something the scroll can never give. Yes, information will increase. The angel was not wrong about that. But the sealed portions that require our faith will not be unlocked by more processing power from larger data centers.

In verse 9, Daniel was told to seal the scroll and go his way. Sometimes the most faithful response to a vision we cannot fully understand is exactly that: have faith, be discerning, and go on your way.

38

2 Peter 3:3–13

[3] First of all you must understand this, that in the last days scoffers will come, scoffing and indulging their own lusts [4] and saying, "Where is the promise of his coming? For ever since our ancestors died, all things continue as they were from the beginning of creation!" [5] They deliberately ignore this fact, that by the word of God heavens existed long ago and an earth was formed out of water and by means of water, [6] through which the world of that time was deluged with water and perished. [7] But by the same word the present heavens and earth have been reserved for fire, being kept until the day of judgment and destruction of the godless.

[8] But do not ignore this one fact, beloved, that with the Lord one day is like a thousand years, and a thousand years are like one day. [9] The Lord is not slow about his promise, as some think of slowness, but is patient with you, not wanting any to perish but all to come to repentance. [10] But the day of the Lord will come like a thief, and then the heavens will pass away with a loud noise, and the elements will be destroyed with fire, and the earth and everything that is done on it will be disclosed.

[11] Since all these things are to be destroyed in this way, what sort of persons ought you to be in leading lives of holiness and godliness, [12] waiting for and hastening the coming of the day of God, because of which the heavens will be set ablaze and destroyed and the elements will melt with fire? [13] But, in accordance with his promise, we wait for new heavens and a new earth, where righteousness is at home.

38

2 Peter 3:3–13

AI at the End of Time

Douglas Estes

In *Star Trek IV: The Voyage Home*, the resurrected Spock completes his training on a trilateral computer interface. The computer verbally examines Spock to help him audit his technical knowhow so that he can rejoin Starfleet. The computer represents a 1980s version of future artificial intelligence (AI)—the questions it asks are discrete and do not build on one another. This is in contrast to contemporary AI systems capable of evolving subsequent questions based on responses from their human dialogue partner. The scene with Spock ends when all three prompts ask him repetitiously, "How do you feel?" Feelings, of course, are not logical, unlike Vulcans.

The last chapter of 2 Peter depicts the coming destruction and renewal of the universe in the starkest apocalyptic sense of any passage in the New Testament. Because it occurs in 2 Peter, it is rarely read, overshadowed by the Olivet Discourse, 1 Thessalonians, and Revelation. The discussion of the coming cataclysm in 2 Peter 3 is complex, but there are three highpoints:

First, Peter wants his readers to know that *scoffers*—argumentative people full of ridicule and scorn—will appear when the end is nigh. These scoffers will make merry even as they make fun of those who believe God plans to wrap everything up and bring justice to the world.

Second, Peter describes what the end of the world will look like. He explains what God did once he will do again, except with a different element—fire, this time, not water. To do this Peter incorporates Stoic cosmological ideas that portray the world ending with a roar.[1] He even includes onomatopoeia for his readers to hear the destruction.[2] He does this to build a foundation for the topic with his audience. If we update cosmological theories, what Peter describes is the Big Crunch; the reversal of the Big Bang as God contracts the universe into itself and all of the elements that comprise the universe will melt into a "hot quantum soup."[3] All to make way for "a new heaven and a new earth" (2 Peter 3:13).

Third, Peter asks his readers how the realization that God will end the world should change the way they live. Peter suggests that this knowledge should spur them on to holiness and godliness. The time frame is irrelevant; Christians may be impatient for the end, but God is patient for the souls still to come to repentance.[4]

Unlike what we have learned watching sci-fi movies, AI does not seem to hasten or cause the end of the world, at least from Peter's perspective. We can still read 2 Peter, though, and ask what it can teach us about this AI moment.

I recently participated in a workshop sponsored by a major AI company that wants to help faculty in higher education be more effective. Like Spock, I agreed as part of the process to chat with the AI in order for it to assess my teaching context. Unlike Spock, I was asked many dozens of narrowing questions that sought to probe myopic details of my approach. (At the end there was no broad "How do you feel?" but after an hour of being mercilessly probed, I refused to answer any more questions). It is too facile to assume that the scoffers are AI. No, there have always been scoffers in general, and this scoffing will continue until the last days. The scoffers that appear at that point in history are those who attack the Christian view cosmologically and eschatologically. If 2 Peter is any clue, they will not be unintelligent. They will exploit the skepticisms embedded in pre-trained AI models and train on biased neural networks, but upon closer analysis their arguments will be driven by their own lusts. The good news is that in those last days, AI-assisted Christians will also continue to make the message of Jesus' return widely known.

There is, however, an eschatological weakness inherent in AI, as with any creation. Humans do not create AI models in a vacuum. Every AI system requires some training data, some human nudge, to begin. (AIs can now train other AIs, of course, but the first AI still had a human launch). AI models will in the future be quite adept at summarizing the sum and total of human knowledge—and I believe—pushing humanity far outside of what it knows or believes it can know. It will run its own tests, research its own data, and reach new conclusions undreamt by people today. Yet AI is a creation occurring within the four-dimensional manifold of Minkowski spacetime. Thus, it has limits. For people, created beings, are ants in a jar, and while we may live in the jar, we are limited to where we can go in the jar in both time and space. Future AI may not have as many limitations as we do now, but there is one limitation it will always have: AI cannot leave the jar.[5] It can never know God's plans, it cannot see before the Big Bang or beyond the Big Crunch, it will forever be tainted by *creation*. It began with a push from humans and that is an AI model's defining vector. The world will end and AI will never know until it does.

While we cannot know the day, we can look forward to the day by taking part in a human version of this future divine purification—striving to be holy, godly, without a mark, and at peace with those around us, and as we wait the patience of God is the sign of his coming salvation (2 Pet 3:15). The blessing of AI is that it can assist us to do those very things, especially if we are willing to allow AI to audit our theological knowhow and probe our ministry contexts. We will be led by our hope of future renewal, and scoffers by their desires. In which case, the scoffers won't stand a chance.

39

Revelation 7:9–17

9 After this I looked, and there was a great multitude that no one could count, from
every nation, from all tribes and peoples and languages, standing before the throne
and before the Lamb, robed in white, with palm branches in their hands. 10 They
cried out in a loud voice, saying,

"Salvation belongs to our God who is seated on the throne and to the Lamb!"

11 And all the angels stood around the throne and around the elders and the four
living creatures, and they fell on their faces before the throne and worshiped
God, 12 singing,

"Amen! Blessing and glory and wisdom
and thanksgiving and honor
and power and might
be to our God forever and ever! Amen."

13 Then one of the elders addressed me, saying, "Who are these, robed in white, and
where have they come from?" 14 I said to him, "Sir, you are the one who knows."
Then he said to me, "These are they who have come out of the great ordeal; they
have washed their robes and made them white in the blood of the Lamb.

15 For this reason they are before the throne of God
    and worship him day and night within his temple,
    and the one who is seated on the throne will shelter them.
16 They will hunger no more and thirst no more;
    the sun will not strike them,
    nor any scorching heat,
17 for the Lamb at the center of the throne will be their shepherd,
    and he will guide them to springs of the water of life,
and God will wipe away every tear from their eyes."

39

Revelation 7:9–17

From *Any* Nation: Artificial Intelligence and Good News for the Great Crowd of the Lamb

Melanie Dzugan

There is a missiological hope that AI will hasten the return of Christ. If we use AI to finally reach the multitudes and translate Scripture for "every nation, tribe, people, and language," Christ can return and at long-last wipe away our tears. Translation is an undeniably tricky issue requiring specialization and cooperation that is slow, difficult, and often, dangerous. However, with the help of AI as a translation specialist, the return of Christ may prove to come soon and very soon, indeed. Of course, we do not know the hour of Christ's coming and much less may we presume to technologically control Christ's coming. Still, a hope lingers that AI may offer a good way to participate in God's mission to reach the ends of the earth with the gospel.

The People of the Lamb

In Revelation 7, the people of God come from *any*where. The author of Revelation sums its drama as a battle between two cities: "Babylon, whoring after power, and Jerusalem, the eternal city."[1] Jerusalem, of course, represents the people of God, but this symbolism does not limit the people of God to one nation (Israel). Here in Revelation, the seer finds a number of 144,000 who bear the twin names of the Lamb and his Father on their foreheads. This crowd of people of symbolic number is described as perfect, pure, truth-tellers, and witnesses—people living the way of the Lamb (Rev 14:4–5). This scene recalls a similar one in Ezekiel 9, where the inhabitants of Jerusalem who "groan over all the abominations that are committed in it" are marked on their foreheads so that they will be protected.[2]

When the seer looks again, however, he sees not a finite number like 144,000 but an *infinite* "great multitude that no one could count, from every nation, from all tribes and peoples and languages, standing before the throne and before the Lamb, robed in white" (7:9–10). This is what it means for Jerusalem to be the eternal city. The theological significance of the great multitude is not so much that the people of God are *every*where but *any*where, forever. Christian thinking and behaving should be motivated by practicing the way of the Lamb who stands in solidarity with the world rather than checking every nation off a translation list as fulfillment of the *missio Dei*.[3]

On Earth as It Is in Heaven

The *missio Dei* is wholly concerned with the good of this world and the "abominations that are committed in it." Palm branches. Blistering sun. Life-giving springs. Despite Revelation's apocalyptic and cosmic imagery, passages like Rev 7 remind us that the *missio Dei* is creation focused. In contrast to Tim LaHaye's image of a people swept up into heaven, in Revelation, we find an image of heaven swinging low.[4] God cares about this earth and all its nations. N.T. Wright makes it clear: "Unlike many hymns and prayers, much iconography, and enormous unquestioned popular assumption, the final scene of the Christian Bible is not about humans leaving this earth and going up to a place called 'heaven.' It is about the heavenly city coming down to earth."[5]

The Christian gospel must be spread as good news here and now for all the earth. The data centers required to support AI's tremendous power demand are notoriously detrimental to the Earth and to the (often poor) communities they neighbor. With respect to data, Levi Checketts compellingly explains that "as currently designed, not only will AI systems be unable to articulate the 'intelligence' of the poor, but worse—they will serve to further marginalize the experience and embodied truth of those worst off in our society."[6] These are who the great crowd before the throne of God represent. They wave palm branches and rely on the Lamb alone for their justification, whose way is of peace and not power. *This is the reason,* verse 15 insists, "they are before the throne of God," sheltered and comforted in New Creation.

Conclusion: Emigrating Babylon

There may yet be hope. Checketts himself offered that to "the degree that AI can be developed to speak with the otherwise voiceless, correct wrongs entrenched in our social structures, and build bridges of understanding and reconciliation between the powerful and oppressed, it can and should be endorsed."[7] Wycliffe uses AI in some impressive ways that protect the work of missionaries and translators working in deeply embodied solidarity with specific and local needs.[8] Any reading of Revelation 7:9–17, however, should caution us not to find ourselves on the side of power in an effort to bring about the eschaton but among the crowd of the world's nations, *any*one who comes from great hardship and whose robes are washed in the blood of the Lamb who suffers with them.

40

Revelation 22:16–21

16 "It is I, Jesus, who sent my angel to you with this testimony for the churches. I am the root and the descendant of David, the bright morning star."

17 The Spirit and the bride say, "Come."
And let everyone who hears say, "Come."
And let everyone who is thirsty come.
Let anyone who wishes take the water of life as a gift.

18 I warn everyone who hears the words of the prophecy of this book: if anyone
adds to them, God will add to that person the plagues described in this book; 19 if
anyone takes away from the words of the book of this prophecy, God will take
away that person's share in the tree of life and in the holy city, which are described
in this book.

20 The one who testifies to these things says, "Surely I am coming soon."

Amen. Come, Lord Jesus!

21 The grace of the Lord Jesus be with all the saints. Amen.

40

Revelation 22:16–21
AI and the Antichrist

Douglas Estes

Is artificial intelligence (AI) the antichrist? Or more precisely, the "little beast" that speaks with the authority of the antichrist (Rev 13:11–12; Dan 7:8)? According to one popular and pervasive myth, AI is the second beast that arises out of the earth—the false prophet, the mouthpiece of the antichrist. It speaks "like a dragon," acts with the authority of the beast, and it does the miraculous to deceive people (Rev 13: 12–14). One of the little beast's miraculous acts is to make an image of the beast come alive (Rev 13:15). Another is to force people to receive a mark in order to legally engage in commerce (Rev 13:16–17).

Even as there is a myriad of proposed interpretations of John's vision, there is also a myriad of reasons why this "little beast" is not AI—or at least, not literally AI. We will take a broad approach rather than a narrow one into this issue.

To understand Revelation, we must start with its very first words: "The revelation of Jesus Christ" (Rev 1:1). The subject of the opening clause, *apokalypsis*, is often rendered as "revelation" but it can also be rendered "apocalypse" (both are accurate). John claims that what follows is an apocalypse, and to some degree he describes the genre—or type of writing—for his audience. This category of writing already existed in the ancient world at the time of his writing, although many scholars consider John's take on the genre unique. Thus, we could be tempted to label John's Revelation as *apocalyptic*—except that this is not the sense with which we use that word today. Starting in the early medieval period, the meaning of apocalyptic evolved into "social movements, predicated on a past prophecy with a vivid imagining of a dystopian future/end-of-the-world scenario believed to be at hand, which frequently brings violence to other people."[1]

For example, it is common to hear people describe climate change as "apocalyptic." These people do not mean, "of or relating to texts of visions in the ancient world," but rather a social movement predicting a dystopian future that requires socio-political action.[2] This evolved definition of apocalyptic bleeds over into thought about AI. Much of the light and heat surrounding AI is due to social interpretations of AI (including by its own pioneers), fueled in no little part by sci-fi movies such as *2001: A Space Odyssey* and *Terminator*. In these cases, AI enters into the socio-technological imagination that induces a feeling that we are in a dystopian future/end of the world scenario. Once people begin to see AI as apocalyptic, it is a small step to see AI as an element of the apocalypse. But this *is* science fiction, not biblical revelation.

If we rewind a little more than two hundred years, for example, writers identified the "little beast" as political figures such as Charles-Maurice de Talleyrand (the mouthpiece of Napoleon) or religious groups such as the Church of England.[3] In fact, it seems as every generation wants to identify the antichrist as some figure within their own context, from Nero to Hitler to AI. Part of the confusion stems from the absence of the antichrist in Revelation. The antichrist only appears in 1 John and 2 John, while Revelation contains mythical metaphors for God's enemies, notably the dragon (identified as Satan, Rev 12:9), the beast, and the little beast. First and Second John is the closest we come to a description of the antichrist—a person or people who stand against Christ (1 John 2:18, 22, 4:3, and 2 John 1:7), usually through deception. Related metaphors for false prophets in other New Testament texts could be unnamed echoes of the antichrist (e.g., 2 Thess 2:3–12; Matt 24:24). In sum, what we know about the antichrist is very little—but we do know AI cannot be the antichrist, as it is not "a person or people."

Some may feel this argument rests on a technicality. Yes, AI is not technically a person, but it talks like a person, and in the near future it will listen, talk, and look like a person (at least on a screen). If John or another ancient saw AI it would appear to them as a person. However, this isn't a technicality as much as it is an admission: antichrists are people who will leverage whatever technology they can in order to oppose Christ. If the antichrist came during the Imperial period, it would use the *cursus publicus*; if the antichrist came during the Industrial Revolution, it would use the telegraph; if the antichrist comes today, it will use AI. Of course AI is (a tool of) the antichrist. So is every human invention.[4]

As John heads to the climax of his vision, we learn that Jesus' message ("a sharp sword") triumphs over the nations (Rev 19:15), including the image of the beast (Rev 19:20). The dragon is restrained for a thousand years, during which time is the first resurrection (Rev 20:1–6). After the thousand years, John's vision comes to its conclusion.[5] The dragon, the beast, and the little beast (or false prophet) are thrown into the fire (Rev 20:10). What follows is a great judgment (Rev 20:11–15), the revelation of a new heaven and a new earth (Rev 21:1–8), the presentation of the holy city, the New Jerusalem (Rev 21:9–27), the tree of life (Rev 22:1–5), and the confirmation of John's vision (22:6–11). Before the vision ends, John offers a last parting thought: Whatever we do, we cannot add to or take away from this vision.[6]

As time passes, this warning grows louder and louder. In John's day, adding to or taking away from a text was limited to interpersonal conversation, dispatched papyri, and socio-political leverage. Over the last two millennia, the power of mass communication transformed humanity. Using generative AI, we can create a shocking image or compelling speech that people can see or hear on social media around the world. As mass media has shown over the last century, mass misinformation can create antichrists faster than anything John could imagine. Even a fractional divergence of direction or magnitude of a large language model (LLM) vector can add to or take away from the meaning of biblical texts. Adding to or taking away is antichrist, and we as Christians must be on watch to ensure that future AI models speak accurately about the Bible, as he is surely coming soon.

"Amen. Come, Lord Jesus!" (Rev 22:20).

Contributors

Nathan Barczi is a MIT Chaplain and Associate Director and Senior Theologian of the Octet Collaborative, a Christian study center serving MIT. He has served as Associate Pastor at Christ the King Presbyterian Church since 2014, and is a senior fellow of the Center for Pastor Theologians. He holds a PhD in theology from the University of Nottingham and a PhD in economics from MIT. He did his undergraduate work at Stanford University in his native Silicon Valley, and he lives with his wife and their three children in Somerville, Massachusetts.

Andrew Byers (PhD, Durham) is Tutor in New Testament at Ridley Hall, Cambridge, and an Affiliated Lecturer at the University of Cambridge. He is the author or co-editor of seven books, including *TheoMedia: The Media of God in the Digital Age* (Cascade, 2013).

Drew Dickens, D.LS, is a thought leader at the intersection of faith and technology, holding a doctorate from Southern Methodist University and a masters from Dallas Theological Seminary focused on the impact of generative AI on spiritual direction. As the former Director of Content for Abide and founder of Encountering Peace, he has built digital communities serving millions of seekers worldwide. He currently advances this mission through the "AI & Spirituality" podcast, helping people navigate the spiritual implications of a machine-driven age.

John Anthony Dunne is an Associate Professor of New Testament at Bethel Seminary in St. Paul, MN. His research interests lie primarily in the New Testament, the life and letters of Paul (especially Galatians), Christian origins, and second temple Judaism. Within these frameworks he is fascinated by many things, including: theologies of suffering and mortality, ritual practices and participation with Christ, symbolism associated with ancient fermented beverages, critiques of imperial ideology, intertextuality with antecedent texts, and the reception of the Bible in contemporary popular culture.

John Dyer (PhD, Durham University) is Vice President for Enrollment and Educational Technology at Dallas Theological Seminary, where he also serves as assistant professor of theological studies. He enjoys writing, teaching, and creating at the intersection of technology and faith, in books like *From the Garden to the City* and *People of the Screen*, in open source tools for Apple and WordPress, and in faith-theme sites like yallversion.com, bestcommentaries.com, and worship.ai. You can find out more about him at https://j.hn/.

Melanie Dzugan (PhD cand., Fuller Theological Seminary) is an adjunct professor at John Brown University and is completing her dissertation in theology with a concentration in Christian ethics. Her work is shaped by her degrees in science and religion and focuses on biblical hermeneutics, public theology, and ethical formation. She is a member of AI & Faith and has preached and served in church leadership, conference leadership, and organized public events for science, theology, and religion.

R. Daren Erisman (Ph.D., Graduate Theological Union, Berkeley) is Assistant Professor of Computer Science at Minot State University in North Dakota, where he developed a data science program offering courses in artificial intelligence. He holds a doctorate in systematic and philosophical theology and is an ordained minister in the Evangelical Lutheran Church in America. His interdisciplinary research explores comparative theology (Christianity and Islam), science and religion discourse, and the ethical and theological implications of artificial intelligence in the life of the church.

Douglas Estes (PhD, University of Nottingham) is Associate Professor of Religion at New College of Florida in Sarasota, Florida. He has written on the intersection of technology and faith for more than twenty years, from *SimChurch* (Zondervan, 2009) to *Artificial Intelligence for Bible Translation and Interpretation* (T&T Clark, 2026). Douglas is an advisor at AI and Faith and a senior fellow in the Center for Pastor Theologians. In his spare time he also contributes research to biblical studies and Tolkien studies.

Akosua Frempong, PhD, is the founder of Listening Ear Communications. She is an adjunct professor at Regent University, Virginia, as well as a member of the Evangelical Press Association. Additionally, her interest in AI has led her to train Christian publishers on the technology and the ethics surrounding it, helping them to ensure they use it to honor God and for His glory.

Ed Gerber is the University Chaplin and Director of Campus Ministries at Trinity Western University in Langley British Columbia, Canada. He is a senior fellow with the Centre for Pastor Theologians and author of *The Scriptural Tale in the Fourth Gospel: With Particular Reference to the Prologue and a Syncretic (Oral and Written) Poetics* (2017).

Jay Kranda is the Innovative Tech Pastor at Saddleback Church. He is a graduate of Biola University and Talbot School of Theology. He is author of *Online Church Is Not the Answer: Beyond Just Streaming to Hybrid Disciple Making* (2024).

Bart J. Koet studied philosophy, theology, and biblical studies in Amsterdam and biblical studies in Rome. He worked in various pastoral contexts (for example, as a prison chaplain) and as a lecturer at various universities. He eventually became a professor of New Testament and a professor of early Christian literature at the Tilburg School of Catholic Theology (Tilburg University, the Netherlands).

Todd Korpi (DMiss, Fuller Theological Seminary) is Missiologist in Residence at OneHope and director of the Digital Mission Consortia at the Wheaton College Billy Graham Center. Todd also teaches missiology and Christian leadership at Fuller Seminary and is Dean of digital ministry programs at Ascent College. His books include *AI Goes to Church* (IVP, 2025), *Your Daughters Shall Prophesy* (Wipf & Stock, 2023), and *The Life-Giving Spirit* (Urban Loft, 2017). He lives in Chicagoland with his family and is committed to equipping the local church to live as a mobilized, mission-shaped community.

James F. McGrath is the Clarence L. Goodwin Professor of New Testament Language and Literature at Butler University in Indianapolis. In addition to his expertise in New Testament, he also works on the intersection of religion with artificial intelligence both in its real-world form and in science fiction. He is the author (together with computer scientist Ankur Gupta) of *Real Intelligence: Teaching in the Era of Generative AI* (PALNI Open Press, 2025).

Carey Nieuwhof is a best-selling author, speaker, pastor, former attorney, and podcaster whose work has equipped millions of leaders worldwide. He hosts The Carey Nieuwhof Leadership Podcast, which is in the top 0.1% of all podcasts in the world, and is the founder of The Art of Leadership Academy, where thousands of leaders grow every month. Across platforms, Carey's content is accessed more than 3 million times per month by leaders, and his books, including *At Your Best, Didn't See It Coming,* and the forthcoming *AI and the Future Church,* offer practical strategies for growth and resilience.

Ken M. Penner, PhD, is a professor of Religious Studies at St. Francis Xavier University in Nova Scotia, where he specializes in applying digital methods to ancient Jewish texts. Past board member of the Text Encoding Initiative, he now serves on the Researcher Council of the Digital Research Alliance of Canada. His work includes co-directing the Online Critical Pseudepigrapha and Brill's series, Digital Biblical Studies.

Clint Schnekloth is the pastor of Good Shepherd Lutheran Church in Fayetteville, Arkansas. He is the author *Mediating Faith: Faith Formation in a Transmedia Era* (Fortress, 2014), and most recently of *A Guidebook to Progressive Church* (2024). He blogs at his Substack, Lutheran Confessions. Much of his work centers in connecting faith community to social service such as shelter, refugee resettlement, and LGBTQIA+ inclusion.

Marcus Schwarting (PhD, CS, University of Chicago) is the senior editor of AI and Faith and an AI researcher at SUNY Buffalo. His research is focused on applying ML/AI to problems in chemistry and materials science. His technical work has been published at venues including *Nature Scientific Data, NeurIPS,* and the *Journal of Chemical Physics.* His work on AI ethics has been published in *Christianity Today,* the *Journal of Theology and Science,* and the *Journal of Lutheran Ethics.*

Jacob Shatzer is a theologian, author, and fourth-generation Chicago Cubs fan. As Provost and Vice President of Academic Affairs he has the privilege of serving the stellar faculty of Union University as they work together to provide students with transformative, Christ-centered higher education across a wide variety of academic programs and fields.

Brian Sigmon is the CEO of Friendship Press, an ecumenical Christian publisher pursuing faith for a better future. Friendship Press is supported by the National Council of Churches (NCC) and manages the NRSVue and RSV Bible translations. Brian has a PhD in biblical studies from Marquette University and a MDiv from Duke Divinity School. Brian is also a science fiction writer, and his 2023 novella *MessiahBot* imagines God becoming incarnate as a chatbot.

James Spencer earned his PhD in Theological Studies–Old Testament from Trinity Evangelical Divinity School. He is President of the D. L. Moody Center and host of the Thinking Christian podcast. James is also an Associate Research Fellow with the Kirby Laing Centre for Public Theology, and an adjunct instructor at Wheaton College. He writes and speaks on Chrisitan discernment and discipleship and the intersection of faith, media, politics, and technology.

J. David Stark is Professor of Biblical Studies and the Winnie and Cecil May, Jr. Biblical Research Fellow at Faulkner University and a Senior Research Fellow at the Kirby Laing Centre for Public Theology in Cambridge. For more from David, see jdavidstark.com.

A. Trevor Sutton, PhD, serves as the senior pastor of St. Luke Lutheran Church in Lansing, Michigan. Sutton is an affiliate scholar at the Acton Institute, professor of theology at Concordia University (Irvine, CA), and the author of numerous books on technology. He teaches, writes and speaks frequently about technology and the church in a digital age.

S. Joshua Swamidass, MD, PhD, is a physician-scientist and professor at Washington University in St. Louis, where he leads research at the intersection of artificial intelligence, biology, and medicine. He is the author of *The Genealogical Adam and Eve* (IVP, 2021) and a fellow of the American Association for the Advancement of Science and of AI and Faith. His work bridges innovative science with broader questions of faith, ethics, and human identity.

Nicole L. Tilford is an independent scholar living in Atlanta, Georgia. She is the author of *Sensing World, Sensing Wisdom: The Cognitive Foundation of Biblical Metaphors* (SBL

Press, 2017) and coeditor of *Biblical Themes in Science Fiction* (SBL Press, 2023). She has also published articles on the reception history of the Bible and apocalyptic themes in AI narratives.

Andrew Witt (PhD, Wycliffe College, Toronto) is Associate Professor of Biblical Studies & Theology at Tyndale University in Toronto, ON, Canada. His research is primarily in the book of Psalms, authoring several articles and a monograph entitled *Voice Without End: The Role of David in Psalms 3–14* (Eisenbrauns, 2021).

Notes

Introduction

1. Marcus Schwarting, "Why We're Desperate to Measure Intelligence," *Christianity Today*, July/August 2025.

2. Stuart J. Russell, *Artificial Intelligence: A Modern Approach* (Pearson, 2010).

3. Ewa Luger, *What Do We Know and What Should We Do About AI?* (Sage, 2023), 4.

4. Marcus Schwarting, "The Technical and Ethical Challenges of Generative Model Alignment," *Journal of Lutheran Ethics* 24.4 (2024).

5. For one example, relying on the work of Richard Hays and Ruben Zimmermann, see Douglas Estes, "AI in the Bible? A Way Forward," in *Artificial Intelligence for Bible Translation and Interpretation*, ed. Douglas Estes (T&T Clark, 2026).

1. Moses at the Prompt

1. Marc Jeannerod, in the foreword to *What Should We Do with Our Brain?* by Catherine Malabou, Perspectives in Continental Philosophy (Fordham University Press, 2008), xi–xiv.

2. Catherine Malabou, *What Should We Do with Our Brain?* Perspectives in Continental Philosophy (Fordham University Press, 2008), 6–8.

3. Charlie Campbell, Andrew R. Chow, and Billy Perrigo, "The Architects of AI are Time's 2025 Person of the Year," *Time Magazine*, December 11, 2025.

4. *Ephphatha*: Openness and AI

1. "Openness" is not the same as "pliable." The church father Jerome (347–420 CE) argues that pliability is a vice; see Douglas Estes, "Virtue Before Knowledge: *Docilis* as Vice in Jerome," *Journal of Ethics in Antiquity and Christianity* 2 (2020): 78–82.

2. It is the bystanders who bring the person to Jesus. Mark vividly and in detail describes how Jesus sets the person apart from the crowd and takes them aside. Pastoral care is thus guaranteed!

3. Hanna J. Lucas, *Sensing the Sacred: Recovering a Mystagogical Vision of Knowledge and Salvation* (Cascade, 2023), 21–26.

4. Ruth A. Meyers, "Christian Initiation," in *T&T Clark Handbook of Sacraments and Sacramentality*, ed. Martha Moore-Keish and James W. Farwell (T&T Clark, 2023), 163.

5. On technological senescence, see Douglas Estes, "Postdigital Humans: Technology and Divine Design," in *Postdigital Theologies: Technology, Belief, and Practice*, ed. Maggi Savin-Baden and John Reader, Postdigital Science and Education (Springer, 2022), 149, 155, 157.

5. Many Words Make Many Worlds, But Only One Makes Truth

1. Hans-Georg Gadamer, *Philosophical Hermeneutics*, ed. and trans. David E. Linge (University of California Press, 1977), 1, 11, 15–17, 29.

2. Gerard O'Regan, *Introduction to the History of Computing: A Computing History Primer*, Undergraduate Topics in Computer Science (Springer, 2016), 190.

3. "ASCII Character Chart with Decimal, Binary and Hexadecimal Conversions," *European Southern Observatory*, n.d., https://www.eso.org/~ndelmott/ascii.html.

4. O'Regan, *History of Computing*, 249–73; A. M. Turing, "Computing Machinery and Intelligence," *Mind* 59NS.236 (1950): 433–60.

5. Turing, "Machinery and Intelligence," 433–35.

6. Turing, "Machinery and Intelligence," 455.

7. Cf. O'Regan, *History of Computing*, 256; Benjamin Eldon Stevens, "Artifice of Intelligence? Theories of Mind in Ancient Epic," in *Artificial Intelligence in Greek and Roman Epic*, ed. Andriana Domouzi and Silvio Bär, Bloomsbury Classical Studies Monographs (Bloomsbury Academic, 2024), 201–8.

8. Joseph Weizenbaum, "ELIZA—A Computer Program for the Study of Natural Language Communication Between Man and Machine," *Communications of the ACM* 9.1 (1966): 36–45.

9. Weizenbaum, "ELIZA," 43; contra O'Regan, *History of Computing*, 258.

10. E.g., Weizenbaum, "ELIZA," 36–37.

11. Cf. Weizenbaum, "ELIZA," 43.

12. Weizenbaum, "ELIZA," 42.

13. Cf. Gadamer, *Philosophical Hermeneutics*, 17.

6. Made in Whose Image?

1. Gen 2:15 reframes the Gen 1:28 "rule over" language considerably. God places humanity in the garden "to work it and keep it," using the Hebrew words *ʿābad* ("to serve") and *šāmar* ("to guard or protect"), servant words, not conqueror words.

9. What Is Man? Placing AI within God's Created Hierarchy, and Responding Righteously

1. Thanks to my colleagues Megan Murphy and Stephanie Hawley for helpful comments on an early draft.

2. Robert Alter, *The Hebrew Bible: A Translation with Commentary*, vol. 3, *The Writings* (Norton, 2019), 39.

3. Alter, *Hebrew Bible*, 39n5.

4. Alter, *Hebrew Bible*, 39n6.

5. James M. Hamilton, Jr., *Psalms* (Lexham, 2021), 1:153.

6. Hamilton, *Psalms*, 1:155.

7. W. David O. Taylor, *Open and Unafraid: The Psalms as a Guide to Life* (Nelson, 2020), 179.

8. Hamilton, *Psalms*, 1:156.

9. James Johnston, *The Psalms* (Crossway, 2015), 1:95.

10. Taylor, *Open and Unafraid*, 178–79.

11. Taylor, *Open and Unafraid*, 179.

11. The Parable of the Talents

1. ACSTechnologies, "Data-Driven Decisions: Using Analytics to Improve Church Operations and Growth," accessed April 22, 2026, https://www.acstechnologies.com/church-growth/data-driven-decisions-using-analytics-to-improve-church-operations-and-growth/.

2. Richard T. France, *The Gospel of Matthew*, New International Commentary on the New Testament (Eerdmans, 2007).

3. Ulrich Luz, *The Theology of the Gospel of Matthew*, New Testament Theology (Cambridge University Press, 1995).

4. Rowan Williams, "The Authority of the Church," *Modern Believing* 46, no. 1 (2005): 16–28.

5. John Mordechai Gottman and Robert Wayne Levenson, "The Timing of Divorce: Predicting When a Couple Will Divorce over a 14-year Period," *Journal of Marriage and Family* 62, no. 3 (2000): 737–45.

6. Jetli Chung and Jason Teo, "Mental Health Prediction Using Machine Learning: Taxonomy, Applications, and Challenges," *Applied Computational Intelligence and Soft Computing* 2022, no. 1 (2022): 9970363.

7. N. T. Wright, *Matthew for Everyone, Part 2: Chapters 16–28* (Westminster John Knox Press, 2004).

8. Deborah Niederer Saxon, *The Care of the Self in Early Christian Texts* (Palgrave Macmillan, 2017).

12. Vestibule to Vainglory

1. See Horst Balz and Gerhard Schneider, eds., *Exegetical Dictionary of the New Testament,* 3 vols, trans. Frederick William Danker (Eerdmans, 1990–1993), 1435.2, who write "the entire breadth of meaning of Heb. *kavod* is taken over into the Greek equivalent *doxa. Kavod* refers to the weight of esteem and honor which a person, esp. the king (1 Kings 3:13), has. It can be used fundamentally of every person, probably with respect to his or her position within the creation (Ps 8:6) or within the community of mankind, where *kavod* is manifest in a graduated way as rank, dignity, and position of power."

2. John Cassian, *Conferences* 5.7, trans. Edgar C. S. Gibson, in *Nicene and Post-Nicene Fathers,* 2nd ser., vol. 11, ed. Philip Schaff and Henry Wace (Christian Literature Publishing, 1894), book 5, chapter 7.

3. C. S. Lewis, "The Weight of Glory," in *The Weight of Glory and Other Addresses* (Geoffrey Bles, 1949).

4. C. S. Lewis, *The Great Divorce: A Dream* (Geoffrey Bles, 1945).

13. Artificial Intelligence Models Are Tools, Not Oracles

1. For discussion, see Adrienne Mayor, *Gods and Robots: Myths, Machines, and Ancient Dreams of Technology* (Princeton University Press, 2018); Benjamin Eldon Stevens, "Artifice of Intelligence? Theories of Mind in Ancient Epic," in *Artificial Intelligence in Greek and Roman Epic,* ed. Andriana Domouzi and Silvio Bär, Bloomsbury Classical Studies Monographs (Bloomsbury, 2024), 195–214.

2. Quotations of Aristotle come from *Politics,* ed. and trans. H. Rackham, LCL 264 (Harvard University Press, 1959).

3. Paulin Ismard, "Renting Slaves in Classical Athens: Anatomy of a Legal Form," in *Symposion 2019: Vorträge zur griechischen und hellenistischen Rechtsgeschichte (Hamburg, 26.–28 August 2019),* ed. Werner Riess and Kaja Harter-Uibopuu, Akten der Gesellschaft für griechische und hellenistische Rechtsgeschichte 28 (Austrian Academy of Sciences, 2021), 419–35; Mayor, *Gods and Robots,* 93.

4. Parsing responsibility in terms of actions undertaken still, however, allows for exculpatory factors (e.g., genuinely unforeseeable consequences of an action; Deut 19:4–7).

5. Cf. Jason Brooks, Fedora Council, and Fedora Community, "AI-Assisted Contributions Policy," *Fedora Docs,* 24 October 2025, https://docs.fedoraproject.org/en-US/council/policy/ai-contribution-policy/.

6. Cf. Dietrich Bonhoeffer, *Ethics,* ed. Clifford J. Green, trans. Reinhard Krauss, Charles C. West, and Douglas W. Stott, Dietrich Bonhoeffer Works 6 (Augsburg Fortress, 2005), 256–89.

7. Andrey Romanov, "εἷς κύριος and ἡμεῖς in 1 Corinthians 8:6: An Investigation of the First Person Plural in Light of the Lordship of Jesus Christ," *Neotestamentica* 49.1 (2015): 47–74.

8. This principle does not mean that, for instance, Jesus's followers may not legitimately delegate responsibilities. But it does mean that such delegation can never be abdication; delegators remain responsible for what they undertake by their delegation.

9. Hans-Georg Gadamer, *Philosophical Hermeneutics*, ed. and trans. David E. Linge (University of California Press, 1977), 17.

14. Embodiment and AI

1. Susan Dominus, "Never Say Goodbye," *The New York Times Magazine*, June 13, 2025.

2. 1 Corinthians 15 is a long and complex passage, rich in meaning and treating many subjects. For further discussion, Gordon Fee discusses Paul's treatment of the resurrection of Christ, the possibility of bodily resurrection, how the dead will be raised, the necessity of resurrection, and the implications of the resurrection; in his *The First Epistle to the Corinthians*, rev. ed., New International Commentary on the New Testament (Eerdmans, 2014).

3. O'Donovan, *Resurrection and Moral Order*, 19.

4. O'Donovan, *Resurrection and Moral Order*, 14.

15. Paul and the Shape of Mediated Presence

1. F. F. Bruce, "The Colossian Heresy," *Bibliotheca Sacra* 141 (1984): 195–208.

17. The Ten Commandments and AI

1. For a basic introduction to law in the ancient world, see John H. Walton, "Understanding Torah: Ancient Legal Text, Covenant Stipulation, and Christian Scripture," *BBR* 29 (2019): 1–18. A great fuller-length treatment of the topic is in Dru Johnson, *Understanding Biblical Law: Skills for Thinking With and Through Torah* (Baker Academic, 2025).

2. The following is informed by Joshua Berman, "The History of Legal Theory and the Study of Biblical Law," *CBQ* 76 (2014): 19–39.

3. See Terence E. Fretheim, "The Reclamation of Creation: Redemption and Law in Exodus," *Int* 45/4 (1991): 361.

4. See Jonathan Burnside, *God, Justice, and Society: Aspects of Law and Legality in the Bible* (Oxford University Press, 2011), 16.

5. For a wonderful overview see Christopher J. H. Wright, "Preaching from the Law," in *Reclaiming the Old Testament for Christian Preaching*, ed. J. R. Ken Grenville, Paul J. Kissling, and Laurence A. Turner (IVP Academic, 2010), 47–63.

6. See Andrew Sloane, *At Home in a Strange Land: Using the Old Testament in Christian Ethics* (Baker, 2014), 170.

7. John H. Walton, *The Lost World of Torah* (IVP Academic, 2019), 232.

8. See Burnside, *God, Justice, and Society*, 52.

9. For example, see Barbara Steffen, et al., "It's Not the AI—It's Each of Us! Ten Commandments for the Wise & Responsible Use of AI" arXiv (2025). https://doi.org/10.48550/arXiv.2511.15740. Their first commandment: "Foster and protect human capabilities."

19. Our Lives and the Lives of Those Around Us

1. See the careful discussion in Michael LeFebvre, "Torah-Meditation and the Psalms: The Invitation of Psalm 1," in *Interpreting the Psalms: Issues and Approaches*, ed. Philip S. Johnston and David G. Firth (InterVarsity, 2005), 217–20.

24. Best, Not Better

1. See G. K. Beale, *Union with the Resurrected Christ: Eschatological New Creation and New Testament Biblical Theology* (Baker Academic, 2023).

2. J. Richard Middleton, *The Liberating Image: The Imago Dei in Genesis 1* (Brazos, 2005).

3. David Brooks, *The Social Animal: The Hidden Sources of Love, Character, and Achievement* (Random House, 2011).

25. Test Everything

1. Amanda Silberling, "ChatGPT Users Send 2.5 Billion Prompts a Day," *TechCrunch*, July 21, 2025.

2. As Oscar Cullman explains, using an analogy from World War II, "the decisive battle in a war may already have occurred in a relatively early stage of the war and yet the war still continues" in Oscar Cullmann, *Christ and Time* (SCM, 1951), 84.

3. M. Eugene Boring, *I and II Thessalonians: A Commentary*, New Testament Library (WJK, 2015), 14–19; and F.F. Bruce, *1 and 2 Thessalonians*, Word Biblical Commentary 45 (Word, 1982), xxii–xxvi.

4. Andrej Karpathy, "Deep Dive into LLMs like ChatGPT," *YouTube*, November 22, 2023.

5. Maureen Salamon, "Doomscrolling Dangers: Constantly Consuming Distressing News Can Take a Toll on Our Health," *Harvard Health Publishing*, September 1, 2024.

6. Paul teaches this principle in 1 Tim 5:8 about how as a father you have a responsibility to take care of your own household and even relatives.

7. See for example, David B. Olawade, Ojima Z. Wada, Aderonke Odetayo, Aanuoluwapo Clement David-Olawade, Fiyinfoluwa Asaolu, and Judith Eberhardt, "Enhancing Mental Health with Artificial Intelligence: Current Trends and Future Prospects," *Journal of Medicine, Surgery, and Public Health* 3 (2024): 100099.

26. The Digital Wilderness

1. Greg M. Epstein, *Tech Agnostic: How Technology Became the World's Most Powerful Religion, and Why It Desperately Needs a Reformation* (MIT Press, 2024).

28. Responsibility in an Age of AI

1. Christopher J. H. Wright, *Knowing Jesus through the Old Testament* (InterVarsity, 2014).

2. John H. Walton, *The Lost World of Genesis One: Ancient Cosmology and the Origins Debate*, vol. 2 (InterVarsity, 2010).

3. Uluğhan Ergin, "One of the First Fatalities of a Self-Driving Car: Root Cause Analysis of the 2016 Tesla Model S 70D crash." *Trafik ve Ulaşım Araştırmaları Dergisi* 5.1 (2022): 83–97.

4. Dario Amodei, Chris Olah, Jacob Steinhardt, Paul Christiano, John Schulman, and Dan Mané, "Concrete Problems in AI Safety," arXiv (2016): 606.06565.

5. Joseph M. Pierre, Ben Gaeta, Govind Raghavan, and Karthik V. Sarma. "'You're Not Crazy': A Case of New-Onset AI-Associated Psychosis." *Innovations in Clinical Neuroscience* 22.10–12 (2025): 11.

6. Kaitlyn Regehr, Caitlin Shaughnessy, Minzhu Zhao, Idil Cambazoglu, Alfie Turner, and Nicola Shaughnessy, "Normalizing Toxicity: The Role of Recommender Algorithms for Young People's Mental Health and Social Wellbeing," *Frontiers in Psychology* 16 (2025): 1523649.

7. Emily M. Bender, Timnit Gebru, Angelina McMillan-Major, and Shmargaret Shmitchell, "On the Dangers of Stochastic Parrots: Can Language Models be too Big?," in *Proceedings of the 2021 ACM Conference on Fairness, Accountability, and Transparency* (ACM, 2021), 610–23.

30. When Voiceless Idols Speak: Inspiration and Companionship in the Age of AI

1. Victoria Tangermann, "Sam Altman Seems to Imply That OpenAI Is Building God," *Futurism*, Nov 15, 2023; and Cade Metz and Mike Isaac, "Meta is Creating a New A.I. Lab to Pursue Superintelligence" *New York Times*, June 10, 2025.

2. See Greg Epstein, *Tech Agnostic: How Technology Became the World's Most Powerful Religion, and Why It Desperately Needs a Reformation* (MIT Press, 2024); though the Way of the Future Church has now closed, Theta Noir is a new AI cult gaining attention—see Tamlin Magee, "A Cult that Worships Superintelligent AI Is Looking for Big Tech Donors," *Vice*, March 21, 2023.

3. Lance Eliot, "People Will Perilously Assume that AGI and AI Superintelligence Are Supreme Oracles and Majestic Prophets," *Forbes*, July 11, 2025.

4. See, e.g., Marc Zao-Sanders, "How People are Really Using Gen AI in 2025," *Harvard Business Review*, April 9, 2025.

34. The Worship of AI: A Double Tragedy

1. www.nobelprize.org/prizes/chemistry/2024/popular-information.

2. These examples and more appear in an article by Douthat's colleague Joseph Bernstein, "It Makes Sense that People See AI as God," *New York Times*, January 23, 2026.

3. Careful readers may note an objection: what if we are worshiping something sinful? Is that creature still good? For example, what if we are worshiping an online influencer who boasts of his mistreatment of women? Or, to stick to Isaiah 44's focus on something made by humans, what if we worship heroin? In this case, we have to distinguish between the creature itself and the distortion of sin. An influencer is a human being, made in God's image, and so the influencer is good. But if we worship an influencer *because* we want to emulate his abuse of women, then what we are worshiping is his misogyny, the very sin that has horribly marred and distorted his goodness and results in violence against others. If we worship heroin *because* we seek pleasure in its abuse, we worship the degradation of human life. In these cases, we would be worshiping sin itself, which is of course not good. I am grateful to the editors for alerting me to this nuance.

4. Augustine, *Confessions* Book X.27.

36. Presence in Our Work

1. Christopher R. Seitz, *Colossians*, Brazos Theological Commentary on the Bible (Brazos, 2014), 175.

2. Nijay K. Gupta, *Colossians*, Smyth & Helwys Bible Commentary (Smyth & Helwys, 2013), 173.

37. The Sealed Scroll and the Search Engine

1. M. G. Siegler, "Eric Schmidt: Every 2 Days We Create as Much Information as We Did up to 2003," *TechCrunch*, 4 Aug. 2010.

38. AI at the End of Time

1. Douglas Estes, "Elemental Imagery, Stoic Physics, and Jewish Cosmogony: Enargeia, Synecdoche and Conceptual Blending in 2 Peter 3," *Journal for the Study of the New Testament*, forthcoming.

2. Duane F. Watson, *Invention, Arrangement, and Style: Rhetorical Criticism of Jude and 2 Peter*, Society of Biblical Literature Dissertation Series 104 (Scholars, 1988), 133.

3. Andrew Paul, "Scientists Predict the Universe Will End in 'Big Crunch,'" *Popular Science*, October 1, 2025.

4. Cf. Douglas Estes, "World on Fire: Environmental Ethics and the Eschatology of 2 Peter," *Journal of Ethics in Antiquity and Christianity* 5 (2023): 108–14.

5. We assume angels can enter into and leave the jar, though that is not for certain, and much depends on how one interprets the nature of angels.

39. From *Any* Nation: Artificial Intelligence and Good News for the Great Crowd of the Lamb

1. Francesca Aran Murphy, "Revelation ('The Apocalypse of Saint John the Divine')," in *Theological Interpretation of the New Testament: A Book-by-Book Survey*, ed. Kevin J. Vanhoozer (Baker Academic, 2008), 237.

2. Marianne Meye Thompson, "Reading What Is Written in the Book of Life: Theological Interpretation of the Book of Revelation Today," in *Revelation and the Politics of Apocalyptic Interpretation*, ed. Richard B. Hays and Stefan Alkier (Baylor University Press, 2012), 170.

3. For more critique of a consequentialist missiology, see Greg McKinzie, "Mission Between Theory and Practice," in *Missional Life in Practice and Theory: Essays in Honor of Gailyn Van Rheenen*, ed. Christopher L. Flanders and Greg McKinzie (Pickwick, 2024).

4. Jerry B. Jenkins and Tim LaHaye, *The Left Behind Series Complete Set, Volumes 1–16* (Tyndale, 2008).

5. N. T. Wright, "Revelation and Christian Hope: Political Implications of the Revelation to John," in *Revelation and the Politics of Apocalyptic Interpretation*, ed. Richard B. Hays and Stefan Alkier (Baylor University Press, 2012), 106.

6. Levi Checketts, "Artificial Intelligence and the Marginalization of the Poor," *Journal of Moral Theology* 11 (2022): 87.

7. Checketts, "Artificial Intelligence," 109–110.

8. Specifically, see Wycliffe's AI project, Chameleon, at https://wycliffe.org/chameleon.

40. AI and the Antichrist

1. Douglas Estes, "Generating Apocalypse: Artificial Intelligence and Apocalyptic Literature," in *Artificial Intelligence for Bible Translation and Interpretation*, ed. Douglas Estes (T&T Clark, 2026), 247; and for its development in theological traditions, see Peter J. Leithart, *Revelation 1–11*, International Theological Commentary (T&T Clark, 2018), 58.

2. For example, Peter Brannen, "Our Almost-Apocalyptic Climate Future," *The Atlantic*, November 23, 2025.

3. Robert Fuller, *Naming the Antichrist: The History of an American Obsession* (Oxford University Press, 1995), 52–53.

4. If Jesus returns during the age of AI, he may use AI also, even as he used various technologies prior to his death (e.g., boats, roads, and writing). For example, John explains Jesus' victory will come from his mouth (his message), described as a "sharp sword" (Rev 19:15). Both the image of the beast and the sharp sword are forms of communication.

5. The earliest commentary on Revelation by Victorinus of Pettau starts the final chapter of the text at Rev 20:7; see Douglas Estes, "The Last Chapter of Revelation? Narrative Design at the End of the Apocalypse," *Criswell Theological Review* 17 (2019): 97–110.

6. Scholars debate as to whether this warning applies only to Revelation or all the texts of the Bible.

Scripture Index

Subject Index